P9-BXX-150

THE
BROTHERS
LIONHEART

Also available from Purple House Press

Mio, My Son by Astrid Lindgren

THE
BROTHERS
LIONHEART

BY ASTRID LINDGREN

Illustrated by Ilon Wikland

Translated by Jill Morgan

Published by
Purple House Press
PO Box 787, Cynthiana, Kentucky 41031
www.PurpleHousePress.com

Copyright © 1973 by Astrid Lindgren. Copyright © renewed 2001
by Astrid Lindgren/Saltkråkan AB. English translation copyright © 2004 by Jill Morgan.
First published in Sweden as *Bröderna Lejonhjärta* by Rabén & Sjögren Bokförlag AB,
Stockholm, Sweden. All foreign and co-production rights shall be handled by
Kerstin Kvint Agency AB, Stockholm, Sweden.

Library of Congress Cataloging-in-Publication Data

Lindgren, Astrid, 1907-
[Bröderna Lejonhjärta. English]
The brothers Lionheart / by Astrid Lindgren;
illustrated by Ilon Wikland;
translated by Jill Morgan. —1st ed.
p. cm.
Summary: Two brothers share many adventures after their death when they are reunited in
Nangiyala, the land from which sagas come.
ISBN 1-930900-24-4 (hardcover : alk. paper)
[1. Brothers—Fiction. 2. Fantasy.]
I. Wikland, Ilon, ill. II. Morgan, Jill, 1962- III Title.
PZ7.L6585Bt 2004 [Fic]–dc22 2004002639

Printed in the United States of America
1 2 3 4 5 6 7 8 9 10
First Edition

THE
BROTHERS
LIONHEART

CHAPTER ONE

Now I will tell you about my brother. My brother, Jonathan Lionheart, I want to tell you about him. It's almost like a saga, I think, and also a little, little bit like a ghost story, and yet it's all true. Although it's probably not known by anyone, other than Jonathan and me.

Jonathan wasn't named Lionheart from the beginning. His last name was Lion, exactly like mama and me. Jonathan Lion was his name. My name is Karl Lion and mama is Sigrid Lion. Papa was named Axel Lion, but he left us when I was only two years old. He went to sea and we haven't heard from him since.

But now, what I want to tell you, is how my brother Jonathan became Jonathan Lionheart. And all the strange things that have happened since then.

7

Jonathan knew that I would die soon. I think everyone knew it except me. They knew it at school too, because I stayed at home and coughed and was always sick, and for the last half of a year I haven't been able to go to school at all. All the women mama sews dresses for knew about it too, and it was one of them who talked with mama about it, so that I happened to hear, though it wasn't intended. They thought I was asleep. But I was only lying there and had my eyes closed. And I kept on lying there, because I didn't want them to know that I had heard that horrible thing — that I would die soon.

I was sad, of course, and so terribly scared, and I didn't want mama to notice. But I talked with Jonathan about it when he came home.

"Did you know that I'm dying?" I said as I cried.

Jonathan thought for a little while. Maybe he didn't want to answer, but at last he said:

"Yes, I know."

Then I cried even more.

"How can things be so terrible?" I asked. "How can things be so terrible that some must die, when they're not even ten years old?"

"You know, Scotty, I don't believe it's that terrible," said Jonathan. "I think it'll be wonderful."

"Wonderful," I said. "Is it wonderful to lie under the ground and be dead?"

"Oh," said Jonathan, "it's only your shell that lies there. You fly away to an entirely different place."

"Where to?" I wondered, because I could hardly believe him.

8

"To Nangiyala," he said.

To Nangiyala — he tossed it out as if it were something everyone knew. But I'd never heard talk of it before.

"Nangiyala?" I said. "Where's that?"

Then Jonathan said that he didn't know and it wasn't all that important. But it was somewhere on the other side of the stars. And he began to talk about Nangiyala, so that almost immediately you felt like flying there.

"It's still the time of campfires and sagas there," he said, "and you'll like that."

Nangiyala is where all sagas come from, he said, because things such as that only happen there, and if you went there, then you would have adventures from morning to evening and at night too, Jonathan said.

"You know, Scotty," he said. "It won't be like lying here and coughing and being sick and never being able to play."

Jonathan calls me Scotty. He's done that ever since I was little, and one time when I asked him why, he said it was because he loved biscotti, especially biscotti like me. Yes, Jonathan liked me, and that was strange. Because I've never been anything else but a fairly homely, rather foolish and scared boy, with crooked legs and all. I asked Jonathan how he could like such a homely and foolish boy as me, with crooked legs and all, and then he said:

"If you weren't such a nice, homely little boy with crooked legs, then you wouldn't be my Scotty, the one I like."

But that evening, when I was so scared of dying, he said that if I went to Nangiyala I would become healthy and strong and more handsome right away.

"As handsome as you?" I asked.

"More handsome," said Jonathan.

But he shouldn't try to fool me. Because no one has ever been as handsome as Jonathan and no one ever will be.

Once, one of the women mama sews for said:

"Dear Mrs. Lion, you have a son who looks like a prince from a saga!"

And she didn't mean me, you can be sure of that!

Jonathan really did look like a prince from a saga, he did. His hair glistened like gold and he had beautiful dark blue eyes that really sparkled, and beautiful white teeth and perfectly straight legs.

And not just that. He was also kind and strong, and he knew everything and understood everything and was at the top of his class, and all the neighborhood kids hung around him wherever he went and wanted to be near him. He made up funny things for them and took them on adventures, and I could never go with them, because of course I was lying on my old kitchen sofa day in and day out. But Jonathan told me everything when he came home, everything he had done and everything he had seen and heard and read. He would sit with me as long as I wanted on the edge of my sofa and talk to me. Jonathan also slept in the kitchen, on a bed that he brought out of the closet in the evenings. And when he had gone to bed, he continued to tell me sagas and stories, until mama called out from the other room:

12

"Now you have be quiet! Kalle must sleep."

But it's hard to sleep when you don't do anything but cough. Sometimes Jonathan got up in the middle of the night and boiled honey-water for me to soften my cough. Yes, he was kind, Jonathan!

That evening, when I was so scared of dying, he sat by me for several hours and we talked about Nangiyala, but very quietly so that mama wouldn't hear. She was sewing as usual, she has her sewing machine in her room, the room where she sleeps — we only have one room and the kitchen, you know. The door there was open, and we could hear her singing, that same old song about a seaman far away at sea, maybe it was papa she was thinking about. I don't remember exactly how it goes, I only recall a few lines which go like this:

If I die at sea, my love,
perhaps one evening,
a snow-white dove
flies home to you,
then to your window hurry,
my soul is near
wanting to rest awhile
in arms so dear...

I think it's a beautiful, sad song, but Jonathan laughed when he heard it and said:

"You know, Scotty, maybe you'll fly to me one evening. From Nangiyala. And you'll sit there as a snow-white dove on the window sill, if you're so kind!"

13

began to cough just then, and he lifted me up and
me as he always did, when it was bad, and he sang:

My little Scotty, I know
your soul is here
wanting to rest awhile
in arms so dear...

Not until then did I think about what it would be
like, going to Nangiyala without Jonathan. How lonely
I would become without him. What good would it be
to have lots of sagas and adventures if Jonathan weren't
with me? I'd just be scared and wouldn't know what to
do.

"I don't want to go there," I said and I cried. "I want
to be where you are, Jonathan!"

"Well, of course I'm coming to Nangiyala too, surely
you understand?" said Jonathan. "In time."

"In time, yes," I said. "But maybe you'll live until
you're ninety years old, and during that time I'll be there
alone."

Then Jonathan said that in Nangiyala *time* is not the
same as it is here on Earth. Even if he did live to be
ninety, I wouldn't think that it took more than two days
before he came. Because that's the way it is, when a real
time doesn't exist.

"You can stay alone for two days," he said. "You can
climb trees and make a campfire in the forest and sit by
a little stream and fish, all those things you've longed to
do so much. And while you're sitting there and bringing
up a perch, I'll come flying in and then you'll say: 'What

in the world, Jonathan, are you here already?' "

I tried to stop crying, because I thought I could stand two days.

"Just imagine how good it would be if you'd gone first," I said, "so that it was you sitting there and fishing."

Jonathan agreed with me about that. He looked at me for a while, kindly as he always does, and I noticed he was sad, because he said very quietly and rather sorrowfully:

"But instead I must live on Earth without my Scotty. Maybe for ninety years!"

Yes, that's what we believed!

CHAPTER TWO

Now I'm coming to the hard part. the part I can't think about. The part I can't stop thinking about.

My brother Jonathan, it could be that he was still with me, sitting and talking with me in the evenings, going to school and playing with the neighborhood kids and boiling honey-water for me and all that. But it is not like that...it *is* not!

Jonathan is in Nangiyala now.

It's hard, I can't, no, I *can't* tell you. But this is what it said in the paper afterward:

A horrible, extensive fire ravaged Fackelrosen Block here in town last night, in which one of the old wooden houses was left in ashes and a life was lost. A ten-year-old boy, Karl Lion, was present when the fire broke out, alone and sick in bed, in an apartment two stories up. Immediately after coming home, his brother thirteen-year-old Jonathan Lion, bravely rushed into the burning building to rescue his brother, before anyone could stop him. Within seconds, however, the entire staircase was a sea of fire and because the two boys were shut inside with the flames, the only thing that remained for them to try was leaping out of the window to save themselves. The horrified crowd that had gathered outside the building was forced to witness as the thirteen-year-old took his brother on his back, with the fire blazing behind him, and unhesitatingly threw himself out of the window. In his fall to the ground, the boy was so seriously injured that he died almost immediately. The younger brother, however, protected by his brother's body in the fall, escaped uninjured. The mother of the two brothers was visiting with a customer at the time — she is a dress-maker — and she received a severe shock when returning home. It is unknown how the fire started.

On the other side of the paper there was more about Jonathan. It was written by his schoolteacher. This is what it said:

Dear Jonathan Lion, shouldn't you have really been called Jonathan Lionheart? Do you remember when we read in the history book about a brave English king by the name of Richard the Lionheart? Do you remember what you said then: 'Imagine being so brave that afterward it's in the history books, I could never be like that!' Dear Jonathan, even if you're not in the history books, you were just as brave at the decisive moment, of course you were a hero as great as any other. Your old schoolteacher will never forget you. Your school friends will remember you for a long time too. It will be empty in class without our happy, handsome Jonathan. But the gods love those who die young. Jonathan Lionheart, rest in peace!

Greta Andersson

She's rather silly, Jonathan's schoolteacher, but she thought highly of Jonathan, just like everyone did. And it was good that she came up with Lionheart, that was really good!

There probably isn't anyone in town who doesn't mourn for Jonathan, and who hadn't thought that it would've been better if I had died instead. At least, that's what I hear from all the women who come here with their fabric and muslin and things. They sigh and talk about me when they go through the kitchen, and they say to mama, "Poor Mrs. Lion! And Jonathan who was just so extraordinary!"

Now we live in the house next to our old house. In an apartment exactly like the old one, but it's on the first floor. We got some used furniture from social services, and the women have also given us some things. I lie on practically the same kitchen sofa as before. Everything is practically the same as before. And everything, absolutely everything is different than before! Because Jonathan is not here any more. No one sits with me and talks with me in the evenings, I'm so lonely that my heart aches and I can only lie here and whisper to myself the words that Jonathan said right before he died. When we were lying on the ground after we had jumped. At first he was lying face down, but someone turned him over and I saw his face. A little blood was running out of the corner of his mouth and he almost couldn't talk. But it was as if he were trying to smile, and he said a few words, "Don't cry, Scotty, we'll meet in Nangiyala!"

He only said that and nothing more. Then he

closed his eyes and the folks came and carried him away, and I never saw him again.

The time right after that I don't want to remember. But it's hard to forget something so horrible and painful. I laid there on my sofa and thought about Jonathan until I felt my head would split, no one could miss him as much as I did. I was scared too. Because I kept thinking that everything about Nangiyala might not be true! Maybe it was just one of those funny things that Jonathan used to make up so often! I cried a lot, I did.

But then Jonathan came and consoled me, yes, he came, oh, it was nice! Everything was fine again, almost. He probably realized there in Nangiyala, how I felt without him and he thought that he should console me. That's why he came to me and now I'm not sad any more, now I'm just waiting.

It was one evening a little while ago, that he came. I was alone at home, and I was lying down and crying for him and I was scared and unhappy and sick and miserable, more than I can say. The kitchen window stood open, because it was such a fine, warm spring evening. I heard the doves cooing outside. There are many of them in the backyard, and they coo all the time now in the spring.

Then it happened.

Well, I was lying there and crying with my face in the pillow, I heard cooing quite close, and when I glanced up, there was a dove sitting on the window sill watching me with its kind eyes. A *snow-white* dove please notice, not a gray one like those in the yard! A

snow-white dove, you can't imagine how I felt at first when I saw it. Because it was exactly like in the song — 'maybe one evening, a snow-white dove flies home to you.' And it was as if I heard Jonathan singing it again, 'My little Scotty, I know your soul is here,' but now it was he who had come to me instead.

I wanted to say something, but I couldn't. I just lay there and heard the dove cooing, and behind its cooing, or in the middle of its cooing, or how should I say it, I heard Jonathan's voice. Though it didn't sound as it usually did. It was just a sort of whispering all over the kitchen. This sounds almost like a ghost story and you might have been scared, but I wasn't. I was so happy, I could have jumped to the roof. Because everything that I heard was so wonderful.

Well then, it certainly was true, about Nangiyala! Jonathan wanted me to hurry and get there, because everything there was good in every way, he said. Just imagine, a house stood waiting for him, when he arrived, he had been given a house completely his own in Nangiyala. It's an old farm he said, called Knights Farm and it lies in Cherry Valley. Doesn't that sound wonderful? And just think, the first thing he saw, when he got to Knights Farm was a little green sign on the gate, and on the sign was clearly written: Brothers Lionheart.

"Which means that we'll live there, both of us," said Jonathan.

Anyway, I'll be named Lionheart too, when I go to Nangiyala. I'm glad about that, because I want to have the same name as Jonathan, even if I'm not as brave as him.

"Just come as fast as you can," he said. "If you don't find me home at Knights Farm, I'll be sitting down by the stream fishing."

Then it became quiet and the dove flew away. Right over the roofs of the houses. Back to Nangiyala.

And I'm lying here on my sofa, just waiting to fly after him. I hope it's not too hard to find my way there. But Jonathan said it wasn't hard at all. I've written down the address, for safety's sake:

> Brothers Lionheart
> Knights Farm
> Cherry Valley
> Nangiyala

Jonathan has lived alone there for two months now. For two, long terrible months, I've been without him. But I'm going to Nangiyala, soon now too. Soon, soon I will fly there. Maybe tonight. It feels as if it should be tonight. I'll write a note and set it on the kitchen table, so that mama finds it when she wakes up early in the morning.

On the note it will say:

Don't cry, Mama!
We'll meet in Nangiyala!

CHAPTER THREE

*T*HEN IT HAPPENED. AND I'VE NEVER BEEN PART of anything stranger. Suddenly I was standing in front of the gate, reading the green sign: Brothers Lionheart.

How did I get there? When did I fly? How could I find my way without asking anyone at all? I don't know. I only know that suddenly I was standing there, looking at the name on the sign.

I called to Jonathan. I shouted several times, but he didn't answer. And then I remembered — of course, he was sitting down by the stream fishing.

I began to run. Down the narrow path to the stream. I ran and ran — and there, down by the bridge sat Jonathan. My brother, he sat there, his hair glistening in the sunshine. And if I tried to tell you, I still couldn't say what it felt like to see him again.

He didn't notice that I had come. I tried to shout 'Jonathan', but I think I was crying, because it became just a funny little sound. Jonathan heard it anyway. He looked up and saw me. At first it was as if he didn't know me. But then he shouted out and threw down his fishing pole and came rushing up and hugged me, exactly as if he wanted to make sure that I had really come. And then I cried, only a little. Why should I be crying for that matter, but I had missed him so much.

Jonathan, he laughed instead, and we stood there on the hillside down by the stream and held each other and were happier than I can begin to say, because we were together again.

And then Jonathan said:

"Oh, Scotty Lionheart, now you're here at last!"

Scotty Lionheart — it sounded crazy, so we laughed about it. And we laughed about it more and more, just as if it were the funniest thing we'd heard in a long

time, though it was probably because we just *wanted* something to laugh at, because we were so happy and we were tingling inside. And as we laughed, we began wrestling, but that didn't stop us from laughing. Oh no! We fell down in the grass and we lay there and rolled around and laughed harder and harder, until at last we laughed so hard that we fell down into the stream. Then we laughed so much that I thought we'd drown.

But instead we began to swim. I never could swim, though I've wished so badly to learn how. Now I could, just like that. I could swim easily.

"Jonathan, I can swim!" I shouted.

"Yes, you can truly swim," said Jonathan.

And then suddenly, I thought of something.

"Jonathan, have you noticed something?" I said. "I'm not coughing anymore."

"No, you're truly not coughing," said Jonathan. "You're in Nangiyala now."

I swam around for quite a while and then I scrambled up onto the bridge and stood there, wet with the water running out of my clothes. My pants stuck tightly to my legs, which was why I could see clearly what had happened. Believe it or not, my legs were perfectly straight, exactly like Jonathan's.

Then I thought, and wondered if I'd also become handsome too? I asked Jonathan if he thought so. In case he could see if I'd become handsome.

"Look in the mirror," he said, and he meant the stream. Because the water was smooth and still, so that you could see yourself in it. I lay down on my stomach on the bridge and peered down over the edge and I saw myself in the water, but I didn't notice anything particularly handsome about myself. Jonathan came and lay beside me, and we laid there for a long time, peering at the brothers Lionheart down there in the water, Jonathan so handsome with his golden hair and his eyes and that fine face he has, and I saw too, my bony nose and my scraggly hair and all.

"No, I can't say that I've become handsome," I said.

But Jonathan thought there was a great difference from before.

"And you look so healthy, too," he said.

Then I examined myself properly. I felt, as I lay there on the bridge, that I was healthy and well, every part of me, so why did I need to be handsome? My whole body was so happy that it seemed to be laughing.

We lay there for a while and let the sunshine warm us and we watched the fish swimming in and out under the bridge. But then Jonathan wanted us to go home, and I also wanted to, because I was curious about Knights Farm, where I would now live.

Jonathan walked in front of me on the path up to the farm, and with my fine straight legs I jogged behind him. I went along just staring at my legs and feeling how good it was to use them. But when we'd gone a little bit up the hillside, I suddenly turned my head. And then — then I saw Cherry Valley at last. Oh! The valley, it was white with cherry blossoms everywhere! White and green, it was, with cherry blossoms and green, green grass. And through all the green and white, a river floated like a silver ribbon. Why hadn't I noticed it all before, had I only seen Jonathan? But now I stood still on the path and saw how beautiful it was, and I said to Jonathan:

"This must be the most beautiful valley on Earth."

"Yes, but not on Earth," said Jonathan, and then I remembered that I was in Nangiyala.

All around Cherry Valley were tall mountains, which were beautiful too. And down the mountain slopes, streams and waterfalls flowed into the valley, singing because it was spring.

There was something special in the air too. It felt as if you could drink it, it was so pure and good.

"They could do with a few pounds of this air back at home in town," I said, because I remembered how I used to long for air when I laid on my kitchen sofa and it felt as if there were no air at all.

But here it was, and I breathed in as much as I could. It was as if I couldn't get enough. Jonathan laughed at me and said:

"You can leave a little for me, anyhow."

The path we walked on was white with fallen cherry blossoms, and fine white petals floated down over us, so that we got them in our hair and everywhere, but I like little green paths with cherry blossom petals on them, I really do.

And at the end of the path lay Knights Farm with the green sign on the gate.

"Brothers Lionheart," I read it aloud to Jonathan. "Just think, that we'll live here!"

"Yes, think of that, Scotty," said Jonathan. "Isn't it fine?"

And it certainly was fine. I understood how Jonathan felt. I personally couldn't imagine any other place where I'd rather live.

It was an old white house, not big at all, with green timbers and a green door and a little green lawn all around, where cowslips and daisies grew in the grass. Lilacs and cherry trees were there, too, blooming wildly, and surrounding it was a stone wall, a short little gray wall with pink flowers on it. You could have jumped over it, as easily as anything, but once inside the gate, you felt that the wall protected you from everything outside, it felt as if you were now home and on your own.

By the way, there were two houses, not just one, though the other one was more like a barn or something like that. They lay at an angle to each other, the houses, and just where they met, an old bench stood that almost looked like it was from the Stone Age. A nice bench and a pleasant corner, it was, in any case. You almost felt like sitting there, thinking for a while, or talking and watching the little birds, maybe drinking juice or something.

"I'll enjoy it here," I said to Jonathan. "Is it just as nice inside the house?"

"Come and see," he said. He already stood by the door and was ready to go in, but just then I heard neighing, yes, it really was a horse neighing, and Jonathan said:

"I think we'll go to the barn first!"

He went in the other house and I ran after him, just guess if I ran after him!

It definitely was a barn, just like I'd thought, and two

horses stood there, two beautiful brown horses which turned their heads and neighed at us, when we came in through the door.

"Here are Grim and Fyalar," said Jonathan. "Guess which of them is yours."

"No, don't try," I said. "Don't try telling me that one of these horses is mine, because I won't believe it anyway."

But Jonathan said that in Nangiyala no one could manage without a horse.

"You can't go anywhere without a horse," he said. "And you see, Scotty, you have to travel a long way sometimes."

That was the best thing I'd heard in a long time — that you had to have a horse in Nangiyala, yes, because I love horses. And think how soft their noses are, I can't imagine anything else that's so soft.

They were a pair of unusually beautiful horses, the two there in the barn. Fyalar had a white blaze on his forehead, but otherwise they were exactly the same.

"Then maybe Grim is mine," I said, because Jonathan wanted me to guess.

"Well, you're off the mark," said Jonathan. "Fyalar is yours."

I let Fyalar nuzzle me, and I rubbed him without being a bit scared, although I'd never touched a horse before. I liked him from the start, and he certainly liked me, at least I thought so.

"We've also got rabbits," said Jonathan. "In a cage behind the barn. You can look at them later."

Well, that's what he thought!

"I *must* see them now, right away," I said, because I've always wanted rabbits and at home, in town, you just couldn't have them.

I made a quick little turn behind the barn and three small, sweet rabbits really sat there in a cage, nibbling on some dandelion leaves.

"It's strange," I said to Jonathan after that. "Everything I've wished for is here in Nangiyala."

"Yes, that's what I told you," said Jonathan. And it was definitely as he'd said, when he sat there with me in the kitchen at home. Although now I was able to see that it was true, too, and I was happy.

There are some things you never forget. Never, ever, ever will I forget that first evening in the kitchen at Knights Farm, how glorious it was and how it felt to lie there and talk to Jonathan exactly like before. Now we were living in a kitchen again like we had always done. Though it didn't look like our kitchen at home in town, that much was certain. I think it's probably very old, the kitchen at Knights Farm, with rough beams in the ceiling and its large open fireplace. What a fireplace, it took up almost a whole wall and if you wanted to cook, you needed to do it directly over the fire, just like they did in the old days. In the middle of the floor stood the sturdiest table I've seen in my life, with long wooden benches along the sides and I think at least a score of people could sit there and eat at the same time without becoming crowded.

"It would probably be good if we live in the kitchen like we used to," said Jonathan, "so Mama can have the other room, when she comes."

One room and a kitchen, that was the entire Knights Farm, but we weren't used to more and we didn't need more. It was still at least twice as big as at home.

Yes, at home! I told Jonathan about the note I'd laid on the kitchen table for Mama.

"I wrote to her that we'd meet in Nangiyala. Though who knows when she'll come."

"It may take a long time," said Jonathan. "But she'll have a fine room with space for ten sewing machines, if she wants them."

Guess what I like! I like lying on an old-fashioned bench in an old-fashioned kitchen, talking with

Jonathan while the light from the fire flickers around the walls, and when I look out through the window, I see a cherry tree branch swaying in the evening breeze. And then the fire dies smaller and smaller, until only the embers are left, and the shadows darken in the corners, and I become sleepier and sleepier, and I lie there not coughing and Jonathan talks to me. He talks and talks, until at last I hear his voice just as a whisper again, and then I sleep. That's exactly what I like, and that's how it was the first evening at Knights Farm, and that's why I'll never forget it.

CHAPTER FOUR

*A*ND THE NEXT MORNING WE RODE. YES, I *COULD* ride, and yet it was the first time I'd ever been on a horse — I don't understand how that can *be* in Nangiyala, that you can do everything, I mean. I galloped about as if I had never done anything else.

But to see Jonathan, when he rode! The woman who thought that my brother looked like a saga prince, she should have been with us as he went dashing along on his horse over the fields in Cherry Valley, then she would've seen a saga prince that she'd never forget! Oh, when he came at a full gallop and jumped over the stream, as if flying, so that his hair flowed around him, yes, then you really could believe that he was a saga prince. He was almost always dressed like that, or maybe more like a knight. There was a cabinet full of clothes at Knights Farm, wherever they had come from, and they weren't at all like the ones we have nowadays, but just like knight's clothes. We had picked out some for me, too, I'd thrown away my ugly old rags, and I never wanted to see them again. Because Jonathan said we must dress so that it suited the time we lived in now, or else the people in Cherry Valley would think we were strange. The days of campfires and sagas, wasn't it just as Jonathan had said? As we rode around in our handsome knight's clothes, I asked him:

"Are these terribly olden days that we live in here in Nangiyala?"

"You could say that, perhaps in some ways," said Jonathan. "Certainly they are olden days for us. But you can also say that they are young days."

He thought for a while.

"Yes, that's it," he said, "a young and healthy and good time, that is easy and simple to live in."

But then his eyes darkened.

"At least here in Cherry Valley," he said.

"Is it different in other places?" I asked, and Jonathan said that it certainly could be different in other places.

What luck that we had ended up here! Right here in Cherry Valley, where life was as easy and simple as Jonathan had said. It couldn't be easier or simpler or more fun than on such a morning as this. First you wake up sitting in the kitchen as the sun shines through the windows and the birds chirping happily in the trees outside, and you see Jonathan working quietly and setting out bread and milk on the table to eat, and when you're done eating, you go out and feed your rabbits and groom your horse. And then you ride off, oh, you ride off, and there is dew on the grass that just glitters and shines everywhere, and bees buzzing around the cherry blossoms, and your horse gallops away and you're hardly scared at all. Just think, you're not even scared that it will all suddenly come to an end, as fun things usually do.

Not in Nangiyala! Not here in Cherry Valley, at least!

We rode for a long time over the fields, here and there as they came, then we followed the path along the stream, twisting and turning, and suddenly we saw the morning smoke from the village down in the valley. At first just the smoke and then the whole village with its old houses and farms. We heard roosters crowing and dogs barking and sheep and goats bleating, all the sounds of morning. The village was probably just now waking.

A woman with a basket on her arm came toward us on the path. She was probably a peasant woman, neither young nor old, but a little bit in between and brown-skinned like you become when you're out in all kinds of weather. She was dressed old-fashioned, like in the sagas.

"Oh, Jonathan, your brother has arrived now, at last," she said, with a friendly smile.

"Yes, he's here now," said Jonathan, and you could hear that he thought it was good. "Scotty, this is Sofia," he said then, and Sofia nodded.

"Yes, I'm Sofia," she said. "It's so good that I met you. Now you can take the basket yourselves."

And Jonathan took the basket as if he were used to doing that and didn't need to ask what was in it.

"Take your brother with you to the Golden Cockerel this evening, so that everyone can welcome him," said Sofia.

Jonathan said he would do that, and then we said goodbye to her and rode home. I asked Jonathan what the Golden Cockerel was.

"The Golden Cockerel Inn," said Jonathan. "It's an inn down in the village. We meet there and talk of things we want to talk about."

I thought it would be fun to accompany him to the Golden Cockerel in the evening and see what kind of people lived in Cherry Valley. I wanted to know everything about Cherry Valley and Nangiyala. I wanted to see if it was on target with what Jonathan had said. I thought of a question and I reminded him of it while we rode, before I forgot.

"Jonathan, you said that in Nangiyala you could have adventures from morning till evening, and at night too, do you remember that? But it's so calm here and there are no adventures at all."

Then Jonathan laughed.

"It was only yesterday that you arrived, have you forgotten? Silly, you've hardly had time to stick your nose in yet. You'll have plenty of time for adventures."

And I said, when I got my thoughts straight, that it was adventurous and marvelous enough that we had Knights Farm and our horses and rabbits and everything. I didn't need any more adventures.

Then Jonathan looked at me so strangely, almost as if he felt sorry for me, and he said:

"Well, you know Scotty, I wish that you could have it just like that. Just like that. Because you may know, there are adventures that *should* not happen."

When we got home, Jonathan unpacked Sofia's basket on the kitchen table. There was a loaf of bread in it and a bottle of milk and a little jar of honey and a few crepes.

"Does Sofia supply us with food?" I asked in surprise.

Clearly I hadn't thought about how we would get anything to eat.

"Sometimes she does that," said Jonathan.

"For free?" I asked.

"Free, well, you might call it that," said Jonathan.
"Everything is free here in Cherry Valley. We give to
each other and help each other when it's needed."

"Do you give Sofia something, then?" I asked.

Then he laughed again.

"Yes, but that's not a problem," he said. "Horse
manure for her flower beds, among other things. I look
after them for her — for free."

And then he said quietly so that I hardly heard it:

"I also do other jobs for her."

Just then I saw him take something else out of the
basket. It was a little, little roll of paper, nothing more.
He unfolded it and read what was written on it, and
then he wrinkled his forehead as if he didn't like what it
said. But he said nothing to me, and I didn't want to
ask. I thought he would tell me what was on his piece
of paper when he wanted me to know.

We had an old sideboard in a corner of the kitchen.
And the first evening at Knights Farm Jonathan had
told me something about it. There was a secret drawer
in the sideboard, he said, one you could neither find nor
open if you didn't know the trick. I wanted to see it
immediately of course, but Jonathan said:

"Another time. Now you should sleep."

Then I fell asleep and forgot all about it, but now I
remembered it again. Because Jonathan went over to the
sideboard and I heard some strange little clicks. It wasn't

hard to figure out what he did. He hid the note in the secret drawer. And then he locked the sideboard and put the key in an old mortar that stood high up on a shelf in the kitchen.

After that we went swimming for a while and I dove off the bridge, just think that I dared to! And then Jonathan made me a fishing pole, similar to what he had himself, and we pulled up some fish. Just enough for us to eat for lunch. I got a big perch and Jonathan got two.

We cooked the fish at home in our large fireplace, in a pot that hung on an iron chain over the fire. And when we had eaten, Jonathan said:

"Now, Scotty, we'll see if you can hit a target. You'll need to know that sometimes."

He took me out to the barn and in the tack room there hung two bows. I knew that Jonathan had made them, because he always made bows for the neighborhood children at home in town. But these were larger and nicer, they were certainly fine tools.

We set up a target on the barn door and we shot at it the whole afternoon. Jonathan showed me what to do. And I shot quite well, not like Jonathan of course, because he hit the bull's eye almost every time.

That was funny about Jonathan. Although he could do everything so much better than me, he didn't think that it was something remarkable. He never bragged, but did everything almost as if he weren't thinking about it. Sometimes I believe he almost wished that I would do better than him. I shot a bull's eye one time too, and he looked so glad about it, as if he had gotten a present from me.

When it began to get dark, Jonathan said that now it

was time, now we would visit the Golden Cockerel. We whistled for Grim and Fyalar. They roamed free in the fields around Knights Farm, but when we whistled, they came immediately at a full gallop up to the gate. We saddled them and mounted the horses and then we rode at a leisurely pace down to the village.

Suddenly I felt scared and shy. I was hardly used to meeting people, least of all those who lived here in Nangiyala, and I said that to Jonathan.

"What are you scared of?" he said. "You don't think there's anyone here who would harm you?"

"No, but maybe they'll laugh at me."

I thought it sounded silly when I said it, because why should they laugh at me? But I always imagine those kind of things.

"You know, I think we'll begin calling you Karl now, since you're named Lionheart," said Jonathan. "Scotty Lionheart, it might make them laugh. You almost died laughing at it, and so did I."

Yes, I really wanted to be called Karl. It sounded much better with my new last name.

"Karl Lionheart," I tried out how it sounded. "Here ride Karl and Jonathan Lionheart," I thought it sounded good.

"Though you're my old Scotty in any case," said Jonathan. "You know that, little Karl."

Soon we were down in the village, trotting along the village streets on our horses. It wasn't hard to find the way. Because we heard laughter and talking from far away. And we also saw the sign with a large gilded rooster on it, yes then, here was the Golden Cockerel, just the kind of friendly old inn you used to read about in books. The light was shining so pleasantly out of the little windows. I really felt like finding out what it was like going to an inn. Because I'd never done that before.

But first we rode into the yard and we tied Grim and Fyalar next to many other horses standing there. Jonathan was right, when he said that you must have a horse in Nangiyala. I think every person in Cherry Valley had come riding in to the Golden Cockerel that evening. The pub was crammed with people when we strode in. Men and womenfolk, large and small, everyone in the village was there, sitting and talking and enjoying themselves, though some small children had already fallen asleep on their parents' knees.

How lively it became when we arrived!

"Jonathan!" they called out, "here comes Jonathan!"

The innkeeper himself — he was a large, rosy-faced, rather handsome man — he shouted so that he could be heard over all the noise.

"Here comes Jonathan, no, here come the brothers Lionheart! Both of them!"

He came over and swung me up on a table, so that everyone could see me, and I stood there and felt my face become completely red.

But Jonathan said:

"This is my beloved brother, Karl Lionheart, who has finally arrived. You must be kind to him, as kind as you have been to me."

"Yes, you can count on it," said the innkeeper, and he lifted me down again. But before he let me go, he held me in his arms for a moment and I felt how strong he was.

"We two," he said, "we'll probably be good friends like Jonathan and I. Jossi is my name. Though I'm mostly called the Golden Cockerel. You can come to the Golden Cockerel whenever you want, don't forget that, Karl Lionheart."

Sofia also sat there, at a table all alone, and Jonathan and I sat down by her. She was glad, I think. She smiled so kindly and asked what I thought of my horse and wondered if Jonathan could come and help her in the garden some day. But then she sat there silently, and I noticed that she was worried about something. I also noticed something else. Everyone sitting there in the pub looked almost a bit reverently at Sofia, and when anyone stood up to go, they always bowed first to our table, just as if there were something special about her, I couldn't understand why. She sat there in her simple clothes, with a veil on her head and her brown work-roughened hands on her knees like a common peasant woman. What was it that was so remarkable about her, I wondered?

I had fun there at the inn. We sang a lot of songs, some that I knew and some that I had never heard before, everyone was happy. Or were they? Sometimes I felt that they had hidden problems, just like Sofia. It was as if, now and then, they thought about something. Something they were scared of. But Jonathan had said that life was so easy and simple in Cherry Valley, what were they scared of? Well, at times they were happy, they sang and laughed and all were good friends and liked each other, it seemed. But I think they liked Jonathan the most. It was just like at home in town, everyone liked him. And Sofia, they liked her too, I believe.

Though afterward, as Jonathan and I were going home, we went out into the yard to untie our horses and I asked:

"Jonathan, what's really so special about Sofia?"

Then we heard a gruff voice beside us say:

"Yes, exactly! What's so special about Sofia, I've wondered that for a long time."

It was dark in the yard, so I couldn't see who spoke. But suddenly he stepped forward into the light from the window, and I recognized a man who had been sitting near us inside the inn, the one with red, curly hair and a little red beard. I noticed him because the whole time he sat there looking unfriendly and he didn't sing at all.

"Who's that?" I asked Jonathan, as we walked out through the door.

"His name is Hubert," said Jonathan. "And he knows very well what's special about Sofia."

Then we rode home. It was a cool, starlit night. I've never seen so many stars looking this spectacular. I tried to guess which one was Earth.

But Jonathan said, "Earth, oh, it wanders somewhere far, far away in space, you can't see it from here."

That was a little sad, I thought.

CHAPTER FIVE

*B*UT THEN THE DAY CAME WHEN I FOUND OUT WHAT was so special about Sofia, too.

One morning, Jonathan said:

"Today we're going over to see the Dove Queen for a while."

"That sounds fine," I said. "Who is this queen?"

"Sofia," said Jonathan. "The Dove Queen, I call her that just as a joke."

And soon I would understand why.

It was quite a way to Tulip Farm, where Sofia lived. Her house was on the outskirts of Cherry Valley with the high mountains behind it.

We rode there early in the morning. Sofia stood there feeding her doves. All of her snow-white doves! When I saw them, I remembered her, that white dove that once sat on my window sill, it seemed like a thousand years ago.

"Do you remember," I whispered to Jonathan. "Wasn't it one of these doves that lent you her body the time — when you came to me?"

48

"Yes," said Jonathan, "how else could I have come? Only Sofia's doves can fly through the heavens that far so easily."

The doves were like a white cloud around Sofia, and she stood there so still amidst the fluttering of their wings. Certainly looking like a Dove Queen, I thought.

Then she caught sight of us. She greeted us kindly, as she usually did, but she wasn't happy. She was quite melancholy and immediately said in a low voice to Jonathan:

"I found Violanta dead with an arrow in her chest last night. Up in Wolf Canyon. And the message was gone."

Jonathan's eyes darkened. I'd never seen him like that, never so bitter. I didn't recognize him or his voice either.

"Then it's as I believed," he said. "We have a traitor in Cherry Valley."

"Yes, apparently we have one," said Sofia. "I didn't want to believe it. But now I know that it must be true."

You could see how sad she was, but she still turned to me and said:

"Come, Karl, you should see what I have around here."

She lived alone at Tulip Farm with her doves and her bees and her goats and with a garden so full of flowers that you could hardly make your way through them.

While Sofia went around with me, Jonathan started digging and weeding the way you have to in the spring.

I looked at everything, Sofia's many beehives and her tulips and daffodils and her curious goats, but the whole time I thought about Violanta, whoever she was, who had been shot up in the mountains.

Soon we went back to Jonathan, he sat there weeding and his hands had become dirty.

Sofia looked at him sadly and then said:

"Listen, my little gardener, I think you must get to work on something else soon."

"I understand," said Jonathan.

Poor Sofia, she was certainly more worried than she wanted to show. She went and gazed up toward the mountains, looking around so anxiously. I became worried too. What was she looking for? Who was she expecting?

Soon I would find out. Because suddenly Sofia said:

"Here she comes! Thank goodness, here's Paloma!"

It was one of her doves that came flying in. At first she appeared only as a tiny dot up amongst the mountains, but soon she was with us, landing on Sofia's shoulder.

"Come, Jonathan," said Sofia hastily.

"Yes, but Scotty — I mean Karl," said Jonathan. "He must be told all about it now?"

"Yes, of course," said Sofia. "Hurry, both of you."

With the dove on her shoulder, Sofia ran in front of us into the house. She took us into a little room next to the kitchen and then she locked the door and closed the shutters. I think she wanted to be sure that no one could see or hear what we were doing.

"Paloma, my dove," said Sofia. "Do you have a better message with you today than you had last time?"

She placed her hand under one of the dove's wings and produced a little capsule. Out of it she took a roll of paper, like the one I had seen Jonathan pick up out of the basket and hide in the sideboard at home.

"Read it quickly," said Jonathan. "Quickly, quickly!"

Sofia read it, then she gave a little cry.

"They've taken Orvar too," she said. "Now there's no one left who can really do anything."

She held out the note to Jonathan and when he had read it, his eyes became even darker.

"A traitor in Cherry Valley," he said, "who do you think it is, who could be so despicable?"

"I don't know," said Sofia. "Not yet. But God help him, whoever he is, when I find out."

I sat there listening, and not understanding.

Sofia sighed and then she said:

"You tell Karl. I'll go and make some breakfast for you in the meantime."

And she disappeared out into the kitchen.

Jonathan sat on the floor with his back against the wall. He sat there quietly and looked at his muddy fingers, but finally he said:

"Yes, now you can hear. Now that Sofia said I can talk about it."

He had told me much about Nangiyala, both before I came here and afterward, but nothing like what I was told there in Sofia's room.

"You remember what I said," he began. "That life here in Cherry Valley is easy and simple. It has been like that and it should be like that, but it won't be for much longer. Because when it becomes tough and difficult over in the other valley, then life becomes difficult in Cherry Valley too, you understand."

"Is there more than one valley?" I asked, and then Jonathan told me about Nangiyala's two green valleys that lay there so prettily between Nangiyala's mountains, Cherry Valley and Wild Rose Valley, deep valleys surrounded by mountains, wild, towering mountains which were hard to cross if you didn't know the winding, dangerous little paths, Jonathan said. But the people in the valleys knew the paths and could travel freely to see each other.

"Or more accurately said, they could before," said Jonathan. "No one can escape from Wild Rose Valley now and no one can go in either. Except Sofia's doves."

"Why is that?" I asked.

"Because Wild Rose Valley is no longer a free land," said Jonathan. "Because the valley is in enemy hands."

He looked at me as if he were sad to have scared me.

"And no one knows what will happen with Cherry Valley," he said.

Now I was scared. I had gone around so calmly and thought that there wasn't anything dangerous in Nangiyala, but now I became really scared.

"Who is the enemy?" I asked.

"Tengil is his name," said Jonathan, and he spoke that name so that it sounded terrible and dangerous.

"Where is Tengil?" I asked.

Then Jonathan began to tell me about Karmanyaka, the land up in The Ancient Mountains beyond The Ancient Rivers, where Tengil rules, cruel as a serpent.

I became even more scared, but I didn't want to show it.

"Why can't he stay away in his ancient mountains?" I said. "Why must he come to destroy Nangiyala?"

"Well, you know," said Jonathan. "The one who can answer that, can answer much. I don't know why he needs to destroy everything there is. It's just so. He resents the people in the valleys for the lives they lead. And he needs slaves."

Then he sat quietly again and stared at his hands, but he mumbled something and I heard it.

"The monster, he also has Katla!"

Katla! I don't know why I thought it sounded more evil than anything else that he had said, and I asked him:

"Who is Katla?"

But Jonathan shook his head.

"No, Scotty, I know that you're already scared. I don't want to talk about Katla, because then you won't sleep tonight."

Instead he told me what was so special about Sofia.

"She leads our secret rebellion against Tengil," said Jonathan. "We fight against him, you understand, to help Wild Rose Valley. Though we must do it secretly."

"But Sofia," I said, "why her?"

"Because she is strong and knows things," said Jonathan. "And because she isn't scared at all."

"You aren't scared either, Jonathan," I said. He thought for a little while, and then he said:

"No, I'm not either."

Oh, how I wished that I could be brave like Sofia and Jonathan! But I sat there in the barn so frightened that I really couldn't think.

"Sofia's doves which fly secret messages over the mountains, is this something that *everyone* knows about?" I asked.

"Only those that we can safely rely on," said Jonathan. "But *one* among them is a traitor, and that's enough!"

Now his eyes darkened again and he said so somberly:

"Violanta had a secret message with her from Sofia, when she was shot last night. And if the message has fallen into Tengil's hands, it means death for many over in Wild Rose Valley."

I thought it was terrible that someone could shoot a flying dove, so white and innocent, even if she carried a secret message with her.

And suddenly I remembered what we had in our sideboard at home. I asked Jonathan why we had secret messages in our kitchen sideboard, couldn't that be dangerous?

"Yes, it's dangerous," said Jonathan. "Though it's even more dangerous to leave them with Sofia. Tengil's spies would look there first, if they came to Cherry Valley, not at her gardener's."

That was why it was so good, said Jonathan, that no one knew who he really was except Sofia. That he wasn't just her gardener, but the one closest to her in the fight against Tengil.

"Sofia has decided this herself," he said. "She doesn't want anyone here in Cherry Valley to know, and that's why you must swear to keep quiet until the day when Sofia talks about it."

And I swore that I'd rather die than betray anything that I had heard.

We ate breakfast with Sofia and then we rode home.

There was someone else out riding that morning. Someone we met on the path, just as we left Tulip Farm. The one with the red beard, what was his name again — Hubert?

"So, you've been to see Sofia," said Hubert. "What did you do there?"

"Clearing her garden," said Jonathan as he held up

his dirty fingers. "And you, are you out hunting?" he asked, because Hubert had his bow and arrows in front of him on the pommel of his saddle.

"Yes, I want to shoot a pair of wild rabbits," said Hubert.

I thought of our little rabbits at home, and I was happy when Hubert trotted away on his horse, so that I wouldn't have to look at him any more.

"Hubert," I said to Jonathan, "what do you really think of him?"

Jonathan thought a little.

"He is the most skillful archer in all of Cherry Valley."

He didn't say anything else. Then he urged his horse and we rode on.

Jonathan had taken Paloma's message, placing it in a little leather bag under his shirt and when we got home he put the paper in the secret drawer of the sideboard. But first I got to read what was written, this is what it said:

Orvar was captured yesterday and is now a prisoner in Katla Cavern. Someone in Cherry Valley must have betrayed his hiding place. You have a traitor there, find out who!

"Find out who," said Jonathan, "I wish I could."

There was more to the message but it was written in a secret language I couldn't understand, and Jonathan said that I didn't need to know it. It was only something that Sofia must know.

But he showed me how to open the secret drawer. I

got to open and close it a couple of times. Then he closed it and locked the sideboard and put the key in the mortar again.

The whole day I thought of everything I had learned, and that night I didn't sleep very well. I dreamed of Tengil and of dead doves and of the prison in Katla Cavern, and I screamed in my sleep, waking myself up.

And then — believe it or not! — then I saw someone standing in the dark corner over by the sideboard, someone who became frightened when I called out and disappeared like a dark shadow out through the door, before I'd even really been able to wake up.

It happened so quickly, I almost thought I had dreamed it all. But Jonathan didn't think so, when I woke him and told him about it.

"No, Scotty, it wasn't a dream," he said. "It wasn't a dream. It was a traitor!"

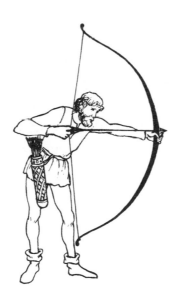

CHAPTER SIX

"*T*ENGIL'S TIME WILL COME ONE DAY," SAID Jonathan. We were lying on the green grass down by the stream, and it was one of those mornings when you couldn't believe that Tengil or any other evil existed in the world. It was completely still and peaceful. The water rippled a little around the stones under the bridge, it was the only thing you could hear. It was pleasant to lie there on your back, only looking at the little white clouds up in the sky and not at anything else. You could lie there and feel good and sing a little song to yourself and not bother about anything else.

And then Jonathan began to talk about Tengil! I didn't want to remember him, but I still said:

"What do you mean? That Tengil's time will come?"

"That what happens to him is what happens to all tyrants sooner or later," said Jonathan. "That he'll be crushed like a louse and be gone forever."

"I hope that it's soon," I said.

Then Jonathan murmured quietly.

"Though Tengil is strong. And he has Katla!"

He said that horrible name again. I wanted to ask him about it, but I let it be. It was good to not know anything about Katla on such a lovely morning.

But then Jonathan said something that was worse than everything else.

"Scotty, you're going to be alone at Knights Farm for a little while. Because I must go away, to Wild Rose Valley."

How *could* he say something so awful? How could he think that I would stay at Knights Farm another minute without him? If he intended to rush straight into Tengil's jaws, then I intended to go with him, and I told him so.

Then he looked at me peculiarly, and said:

"Scotty, I only have one brother, whom I want to protect from all evil. How can you ask me to take you, when I need all of my strength for something else? Something that is very dangerous."

What he said didn't help. My sadness and anger were raging inside of me, and I screamed at him:

"And you, how can you ask me to stay alone at Knights Farm and wait for you and you might never come back?"

Suddenly I remembered how it felt, during the time

when Jonathan was dead and gone from me, and I laid on my kitchen sofa, not knowing for sure if I would ever see him again. Oh, it was like looking down into a black hole when I thought about it!

And now he wanted to leave me again, just disappear into a dangerous situation that I didn't know anything about. And if he didn't come back, then this time there wouldn't be any help, I'd always be alone.

I felt myself becoming angrier and angrier, and I shouted at him even more and said as many spiteful things as I could think of.

It wasn't easy for him to calm me down, even a little. But it's clear that he got what he wanted at last. I knew that he understood everything better than I did.

"Silly, you know I'll come back," he said. That was in the evening, as we sat and warmed ourselves by the fire in our kitchen. The evening before he would leave.

I wasn't mad any longer, just sad, and Jonathan knew it. He was so kind to me. He gave me freshly baked bread with butter and honey on it and he told me sagas and stories, but I couldn't listen. I thought about the saga of Tengil, I began to think that it was certainly the cruelest of all sagas. I asked Jonathan why he had to undertake something so dangerous. He could easily sit at home by the fire at Knights Farm and be happy. But then Jonathan said that it was something he must do, even if it was dangerous.

"Why?" I wondered.

"Otherwise you're not a human being but just a piece of dirt," said Jonathan.

60

He told me what he was going to do. He was going to try to rescue Orvar from Katla Cavern. Because Orvar meant even more than Sofia, and without Orvar it was probably the end of Nangiyala's green valleys.

It was late in the evening now. The embers died down in the fireplace, and night had come.

Then the day came. And I stood by the gate and watched Jonathan ride away into the mist, yes, it was misty over Cherry Valley that morning. And believe me, it nearly broke my heart, to stay there and watch the mist take him, to see how he just faded away and disappeared. And I was left alone. I didn't want to stay here. I went crazy with grief, and I ran into the barn over to Fyalar and jumped up into the saddle and set out after Jonathan. I needed to see him one more time, before I lost him, maybe forever.

He would go to Tulip Farm first, to get his orders from Sofia, that much I knew, so I would ride there. I rode crazy like a fool, and I caught up with him just past our farm. Then I almost felt ashamed and wanted to hide, but he had already seen me and heard me.

"What do you want?" he said.

Well, what did I really want?

"Are you sure you're coming back?" I mumbled. It was the only thing I could come up with to say.

Then he rode up beside me and our horses stood quietly next to each other. Jonathan brushed something away from my cheek, tears or whatever they were, with his forefinger and he said:

"Don't cry, Scotty! We'll meet again — definitely! And if it's not here, then it'll be in Nangilima."

"Nangilima," I said. "Now what's that?"

"I'll tell you about it another time," said Jonathan.

I don't understand how I stood that time when I was alone at Knights Farm and how I passed the days. I looked after my animals, of course. I was almost always in the barn with Fyalar. And I sat for a long time and talked with my rabbits. I fished a little and swam and shot at the target with my bow and arrows, but everything felt so pointless, when Jonathan wasn't with me. Sofia brought food for me, now and then, and we talked about Jonathan. I always hoped she would say, "He's probably coming home soon now," but she never said it. I also wanted to ask her why she hadn't gone to try and save Orvar herself instead of sending Jonathan. But why should I ask, I already knew.

Tengil hated Sofia, Jonathan had explained it to me.

"Sofia in Cherry Valley and Orvar in Wild Rose Valley, they're his worst enemies, and you can be sure that he knows it," said Jonathan, when he told me how things were.

"He has Orvar in Katla Cavern, and he really wants to put Sofia in there too, to pine away and die. The coward, he's promised fifteen white horses as a reward to the person who puts Sofia in his hands, dead or alive."

Jonathan told me that. So I understood why Sofia needed to stay away from Wild Rose Valley. It was Jonathan who had to go there instead. Tengil didn't know about him. At least that's what they thought and hoped. Though someone had understood that Jonathan wasn't just a little gardener. The one who had been in our room that night. The one who I had seen over by the sideboard. The one Sofia couldn't help being worried about.

"That man knows too much," she said.

And she wanted me to get a message to her immediately if anyone else came poking around at Knights Farm. I said that it was no use for anyone to try the sideboard again, because we had moved the secret papers to a new place. Now we had them in an oat bin out in the tack room. In a large tin box lying hidden under the oats.

Sofia went with me into the tack room and dug up the tin box and put a new message in it. It was a good hiding place she thought, and I thought so too.

"Hold out, if you can," said Sofia, as she left. "I know that it's hard, but you must hold out!"

It really was hard. Especially in the evenings and at night. I had terrible dreams about Jonathan and I worried about him every moment I was awake too.

One evening I rode down to the Golden Cockerel. I couldn't stand just sitting at home at Knights Farm, it was so quiet there, my thoughts were too loud. And they weren't thoughts to be happy about.

I assure you that everyone stared at me, when I strode into the inn without Jonathan.

"What now?" said Jossi. "Only half of the brothers Lionheart! What have you done with Jonathan?"

Now this was difficult for me. I remembered what Sofia and Jonathan had preached. Whatever happened, I must not tell anyone what Jonathan was doing or where he had gone. Not to a living creature! So I pretended that I hadn't heard Jossi's question. But Hubert was sitting there by the table, and he wanted to know too.

"Yes, where is Jonathan?" he said. "Doesn't Sofia know what's happened to her little gardener?"

"Jonathan is out hunting," I said. "He's up in the mountains hunting wolves."

I had to say something and I thought this was a good idea, because Jonathan had said there were wolves everywhere in the mountains.

Sofia wasn't at the inn that evening. But otherwise the whole village was there, as usual. And they sang their songs and were happy as usual. But I didn't sing with them. Because for me things were not as usual. Without Jonathan I didn't enjoy it there, and I didn't stay very long.

"Don't look so sad, Karl Lionheart," said Jossi, when I left. "Jonathan will be finished hunting soon, and then he'll come home."

Oh, how I liked him for saying that! He patted me on the cheek and gave me some delicious cakes to take home with me.

"You can nibble on these, while you're sitting at home waiting for Jonathan," he said.

He was kind, the Golden Cockerel. I felt a little less alone because of him.

I rode home with my cakes and sat in front of the fire and ate them. It was a warm spring now, by day, almost like summer. I still needed a fire in our big fireplace, because the warmth of the sun hadn't come through the thick brick walls of our house yet.

It felt cold when I crawled down on my bench, but I was soon asleep. And I dreamed of Jonathan. A dream so horrible that it woke me up.

"Yes, Jonathan," I cried. "I'm coming," I cried as I dashed out of bed. In the darkness around me were echoes of wild cries. Jonathan's cries! He had shouted to me in the dream, he wanted my help! I knew it. I heard him and I wanted to rush right out into the dark night to go to him, wherever he was. But soon I knew how impossible that was. What could I do, no one was as helpless as me! I could only crawl down on my bench again, and I laid there and trembled and felt lost and little and scared and alone, more alone than anyone else in the world, I thought.

It didn't help much when morning came and it was a bright, clear day. Of course it was more difficult then, to really remember how strange the dream was, but Jonathan crying for help, I would never forget that. My brother had called to me, shouldn't I try to go and find him?

I sat outside for hours with my rabbits and brooded on what I should do. I had no one to talk to, no one to ask. I must decide for myself. I couldn't go to Sofia, she would stop me. She wouldn't let me leave under any circumstances, she wasn't crazy. Because it was pretty crazy, I think, could I do it? And it was dangerous too. The most dangerous thing of all. And I wasn't brave at all.

I don't know how long I sat there, leaning against the wall of the barn pulling up the grass. I tore out every blade of grass around me, but I didn't notice until afterward, not while I sat there in torment. Hours passed, maybe I would still be sitting there if I hadn't suddenly remembered what Jonathan had said — that sometimes you have to do things that are dangerous, otherwise you weren't a human being but just a piece of dirt.

Then I decided. I pounded my fist on the rabbit cage so that the rabbits jumped and I said loudly so that it would be certain.

"I'll do it! I'll do it! I am not a piece of dirt!"

Oh, how good it felt after I had decided!

"I know that it's right," I said to the rabbits, because I had no one else to talk with.

The rabbits, yes, they would become wild rabbits now. I picked them up out of the cage and then I carried them in my arms out to the gate and showed them the lovely green Cherry Valley.

"The whole valley is full of grass," I said, "and there are lots of other rabbits you can be with. I think you'll have much more fun than in your cage, only you must be careful of the fox and of Hubert."

All three seemed a little surprised and they took a few small hops as if they wondered whether this could be right. But then they sped away and disappeared and became lost among the green hills.

And quickly I began getting things in order. I gathered what I wanted to take with me. A blanket to wrap around me, when I needed to sleep. A tinderbox to make a fire with. A feed bag full of oats for Fyalar. And a bag of food for myself to eat. Well, I had nothing but bread, but it was the best bread, Sofia's round loaves. She had given me a whole stack and I stuffed the bag full. It would be enough for a while I thought, and when it was gone then I'd have to eat grass like the rabbits.

Sofia would come with soup the next day, she had promised, but by that time I'd already be long gone. Poor Sofia, she'd have to eat her own soup then! But I couldn't let her come here and wonder where I had gone. She would have to know, though not until it was too late. Too late to stop me.

I took a bit of coal out of the fireplace and wrote in huge, dark letters on the kitchen wall:

Someone called to me in a dream, and I'm searching for him far, far away beyond the mountains.

I wrote strangely, because I thought that if someone other than Sofia came to Knights Farm, someone that came to snoop, then he wouldn't know what it meant. Maybe he would think that I had tried to put together a poem or something. But Sofia would understand at once what I meant: I am gone, looking for Jonathan!

I was happy and for once I felt brave and strong. I sang to myself:

"Someone called to me in a dream and I'm searching for him far, far away beyond the mou-u-u-untains," oh, how good it sounded! I'll remember to tell all this to Jonathan, when I find him. I thought.

If I find him, I thought. But if not...

Then my courage fled all at once. I became a little piece of dirt again. A scared little piece of dirt like I had always been. And then, as usual, I longed for Fyalar. I had to get to him immediately. It was the only thing that helped a little bit, when I was sad and anxious. How many times had I stood in his stall with him, when I couldn't manage to be alone? How many times had it comforted me to look into his wise eyes and to feel his warmth and his soft nose? Without Fyalar I couldn't have lived through this time when Jonathan was gone.

I ran to the barn.

Fyalar wasn't alone in his stall. Hubert stood there. Yes, Hubert stood there petting my horse and he grinned when he caught sight of me.

My heart began to thump.

He's the traitor, I thought. I think I'd known it for a while, and now I was certain. Hubert was the traitor, why else would he come here to Knights Farm and snoop?

"That man knows too much," Sofia had said, and Hubert was that man. I understood it now.

How much did he know? Did he know everything? Did he know what we had hidden in the oat bin too? I tried not so show how scared I was.

"What are you doing here?" I said as sternly as I could. "What do you want with Fyalar?"

"Nothing," said Hubert. "I was on my way to see you, but I heard your horse neigh and I like horses. He is fine, Fyalar!"

You can't trap me, I thought and I asked:

"What do you want with me then?"

"To give you this," said Hubert and he held something out to me that was wrapped in a piece of white material. "You looked so sad and hungry last night, I thought maybe you were short of food here at Knights Farm, since Jonathan is away hunting."

Now I didn't know what to say or do. I muttered a thank-you. But I couldn't take food from a traitor! Or could I?

I fumbled with the material and took out a large piece of mutton, it was dried and smoked, the kind that tastes so good, a cold leg of lamb.

It smelled delicious. I wanted to sink my teeth into it immediately. Although I really should've told Hubert to take his mutton and go far away.

Anyway, I didn't do it. It was Sofia's job to deal with the traitor. I, I had to pretend that I didn't know or understand anything. Besides, I really wanted to have that cut of lamb. Nothing would be better in my bag of food.

Hubert was still standing with Fyalar.

"You're really a fine horse," he said. "Almost as fine as my Blenda."

"Blenda is white," I said. "Do you like white horses?"

"Yes, I love white horses," said Hubert.

Then you would want fifteen of them I thought, but I didn't say it. Instead Hubert said something frightening.

"Shouldn't we give Fyalar a few oats? Shouldn't he also have something good?"

I couldn't stop him. He went right into the tack room and I ran after him. I wanted to shout "leave it alone" but I didn't get out a word.

Hubert opened the lid of the oat bin and got the scoop that laid on top. I closed my eyes. I didn't want to see him fish up the tin box. But I heard him swear, and then I opened my eyes and saw a little rat dive over the edge of the oat bin. Hubert tried to kick her, but she ran away across the barn floor, disappearing into a secret hole.

"She bit my thumb, the rascal," Hubert said. He stood there looking at this thumb. And then I took a chance. Quickly, quickly I filled the scoop with oats, and then I shut the lid right in front of Hubert's nose.

"Now Fyalar will be happy," I said. "He isn't used to getting oats at this time of day."

But you're not happy I thought, as Hubert abruptly said goodbye and slipped out through the barn door.

This time he didn't get his claws on any of the secret messages. But it was necessary to find a new hiding spot. I thought for a while and at last I buried the box down in the potato cellar. Inside the door on the left.

And then I wrote a new riddle on the kitchen wall for Sofia:

Red wants white horses and knows too much.
Be careful!

I couldn't do anything more for Sofia.

At sunrise the next morning, before anyone in Cherry Valley had risen, I left Knights Farm and rode up into the mountains.

CHAPTER SEVEN

I TOLD FYALAR WHAT IT FELT LIKE TO BE ME, JUST ME, out for a long ride in the mountains.

"Do you understand what an adventure this is for me? Remember that I've always just laid on my kitchen sofa! Don't think that I've forgotten Jonathan for a single minute. Or else I'd shout, so that it rings throughout the mountains, just because this is so wonderful!"

Yes, it was wonderful, Jonathan would understand that I thought it was. What mountains, just think that they're so high, and that there are so many small clear lakes and rushing streams and waterfalls up in the mountains! And here I sit, Scotty, on my horse looking at it all! I didn't know that anything in the world could be so beautiful, that's why I was completely astounded — at first!

72

But that gradually changed. I found a little riding trail. It was probably the one that Jonathan had talked about. It twisted and curved through the mountains, that's how you got to Wild Rose Valley, he had said. And twist and curve it certainly did. Before long I turned away from the wildflower meadows, the mountains became wilder and more terrible and the trail became more dangerous to move along. Sometimes it climbed up, sometimes it dropped down, sometimes it wandered by rock ledges alongside enormous cliffs, and then I thought I'd never manage! But Fyalar was certainly used to walking on dangerous mountain trails, yes, he was fine, Fyalar!

Later in the evening we were tired, both my horse and myself. Then I struck camp for the night. On a little green patch, where Fyalar could graze, and close to a stream where we could both drink.

Then I made a campfire. For my whole life I had longed to sit by a campfire. Because Jonathan had told me how wonderful it was. And now, at last!

"Now, Scotty, at last you'll know how it feels," I said loudly to myself.

I collected dry branches and twigs in a large pile and lit a campfire that burned and crackled so that sparks flew, and I sat by my fire and thought that it was exactly as Jonathan had said. I felt good as I sat there and looked into the fire and ate my bread and chewed my mutton. It was so good, I just wished that I had gotten it from someone other than Hubert.

I was glad, and I sang a little to myself. "My bread and my fire and my horse! My bread and my fire and my horse," — I couldn't think of anything else.

I sat like that for a while, and I thought of all the campfires that had burned in all the wilderness areas of the world since time began, and how they had died out long ago. But mine burned here and now!

It grew dark around me. The mountains became so dark, oh, how dark it was and how quickly it happened! I didn't like having my back to all that darkness. It felt as if someone could come up on me from behind. Besides, it was time to sleep, so I fed the fire well and said good night to Fyalar and rolled up in my blanket as close to the fire as I could go. And then I wished that I would fall asleep right away, before managing to scare myself.

Well, great! I can scare myself pretty easily. I don't know anyone who can do that as quickly as I can. Thoughts began running around in my head — surely someone was lurking out there in the darkness, and surely the mountains were teeming with Tengil's spies and soldiers, and surely Jonathan had died long ago, my thoughts continued and I didn't sleep.

Just then the moon rose up behind the mountain-top, well, I don't think it was the regular moon, it looked similar but I've never seen moonlight like that before. Of course I've never seen moonlight over tall mountains either.

Everything looked so strange. I was in a mysterious world of only silver and black shadows. It was certainly beautiful and a little sorrowful in a lovely, strange way. But eerie too. Even though it was light where the moon was shining, many dangers could be hiding among the shadows.

I pulled the blanket over my eyes, because I didn't want to see anything more. But then I *heard* something, yes, I heard something instead! A howl far away in the mountains. And then several howls a little closer. Fyalar neighed, he was scared. And then I understood what it was. Wolves were howling.

Someone as scared as I was, could've easily almost died from fright, but when I noticed how anxious Fyalar was, I tried to be brave.

"Fyalar, wolves are scared of fire. Didn't you know?" I said. But I didn't really believe it myself and the wolves hadn't ever heard it either. Because I saw them, closer now, horrible gray shapes came streaking out in the moonlight, howling from hunger.

Then I howled too. I shouted to the heavens. I've never let out such a cry, and I know it frightened them a little.

But not for long. Soon they were back again. Even closer now. Their howls made Fyalar wild. And me too. I knew we would both die, Fyalar and I. I should be used to it, because I had already died once. But then I had *wanted* to, then I had longed for it, and now I didn't want to die. Now I wanted to live and be with Jonathan. Oh, Jonathan if only you could come and help me!

They were so close now, the wolves. One of them was bigger than the others and more brazen. It was probably the lead wolf. He was the one that would bite me, I knew. He circled around me and howled, howled so that my blood froze. I threw a burning branch at him and screamed loudly, but it only annoyed him. I saw his mouth and his terrible grinding teeth that wanted to slash my throat. Now — Jonathan, help! Now he's jumping!

But then! What in the world happened then? In the middle of his leap, he gave a yelp and fell down by my feet. Dead! Absolutely stone dead! And right through his head was an arrow.

From whose bow did this arrow come? Who had saved my life? Someone strode out of the shadows behind a rock. None other than Hubert! There he stood, sneering a little as usual, yet I wanted to rush over to him and hug him, I was so happy to see him. At first. But just at first.

"I arrived just in time," he said.

"Yes, you definitely did," I said.

"Why aren't you at home at Knights Farm?" he said. "What are you doing here in the middle of the night?"

And you? I thought, because now I remembered who he was. What cunning treachery would take place here in the mountains tonight? Oh, why was it a traitor who saved me, why must I be grateful to Hubert? Not just for the mutton, but for my whole precious life!

"What are you doing here in the middle of the night?" I said sullenly.

"Shooting wolves, as you've noticed," said Hubert. "Besides, I saw you when you rode out this morning and it occurred to me that I should see that nothing dangerous happened to you. That's why I followed you."

Yes, just your lies, I thought. Sooner or later you'll have to deal with Sofia, and then I'll pity you.

"Where is Jonathan?" said Hubert. "The one who is hunting wolves should have been here to shoot a few of them."

I looked around. The wolves had vanished, every one. They had probably been frightened when the lead wolf fell down and died. And maybe they mourned too, because I heard sorrowful little howls far away in the mountains.

"Well, where's Jonathan?" persisted Hubert, and then I had to lie too.

"He's coming soon," I said. "He set out after a pack of wolves way over there," I said, and I pointed toward the mountain.

Hubert sneered. He didn't believe me, I noticed.

"Shouldn't you come home with me to Cherry Valley, then?" he said.

"No, I must wait for Jonathan," I said. "He'll probably be here any minute."

"Really?" said Hubert. "You don't say," he said, looking at me strangely. And then — then he pulled out a knife from his belt. I gave a little cry, what was he going to do? As he stood there in the moonlight with the knife in his hand, he frightened me more than all the wolves on the mountain.

He wants me dead, went through my head. He knows that I know that he's the traitor, that's why he followed me and now he wants to kill me.

I began to shake, I was so brave.

"Don't do it," I cried. "Don't do it!"

"Don't do what?" said Hubert.

"Don't kill me," I cried.

Then Hubert turned white with rage. He rushed toward me and came so close that I almost fell backward, I was so scared.

"You little rascal, what are you saying?"

He grabbed my hair and shook me.

"You silly beast," he said. "If I had wanted to see you dead, I could've let the wolves take care of that matter."

He held the knife right under my nose, and I saw what a sharp knife it was.

"I use this to skin wolf hides," he said. "Not to kill dumb kids."

I got a kick on the bottom so that I fell forward. And then he got started skinning the wolf, he swore the whole time he did it.

And I hurried over to get on Fyalar. Because now I wanted to get away from here, oh, how I wanted to get away from here!

"Which way are you going?" cried Hubert.

"I think I'll ride and meet Jonathan," I said, and I heard how scared and frightened I sounded.

"Yes, you do that, muttonhead," shouted Hubert. "Take your own life then, I won't stop you any longer."

But by then I was in full speed away from there and didn't bother with Hubert.

In front of me in the moonlight the path twisted farther up over the mountain. A gentle moonlight it was, but clear, almost like daylight so that you could see everything, what luck! Otherwise I would've been lost!

Because there were steep slopes and chasms that made me dizzy, how horrible it was and how beautiful! It was like riding in a dream, yes, this whole moonlit landscape could only happen in a pretty wild dream, I thought, and I said to Fyalar:

"Who do you think is dreaming this? It's not me. It must be someone else who can dream up something both unnaturally horrible and beautiful, maybe God?"

I was tired and sleepy and could hardly hold myself up in the saddle. I had to rest somewhere for the night.

"Hopefully where there won't be any wolves," I said to Fyalar and I think he agreed with me.

Who had tread up this mountain path between Nangiyala's valleys from the beginning? Who had decided where this path to Wild Rose Valley would go? Was it necessary for it to twist along on such miserable little rocky ledges beside such frighteningly steep slopes? I knew that if Fyalar took so much as one misstep we would fall down, both of us, into the depths. Then no one would ever, throughout eternity, know what had happened to Karl Lionheart and his horse.

It got worse and worse. In the end I didn't dare open my eyes, if we were to plunge into a chasm, then I didn't want to see it.

But Fyalar tread without any missteps. He managed, and when I dared to look again, we had come to a little glade. A fine, green little glade which had sky-high mountains on one side and a deep chasm on the other.

"Here's our place, Fyalar," I said. "We're safe here from the wolves."

And it was true. A wolf couldn't climb down these

mountains, they were too steep. A wolf couldn't climb up out of the chasm, the cliffs were too steep. If a wolf came, it would surely have to use this awful little path along the chasm like we did. But I decided to think that a wolf probably wasn't that shrewd.

Then I saw something really good. There was a deep cleft right through the mountain. You could almost call it a cave, because there were large blocks of rock for the roof. In the cave we could sleep safely with a roof overhead.

Someone had rested in this glade before me. There were ashes left from a campfire. I almost felt like making one too. But I didn't have enough energy. Now I just wanted to sleep. So I took Fyalar by the reins and led him into the cave. It was a deep cave, and I said to Fyalar:

"There is room here for fifteen like you."

He neighed a little. Maybe he longed to be back home in his stall. I asked him for forgiveness since I had dragged him into such hardships, and I gave him oats and pet him and said good night to him again. And then I rolled up in my blanket in the farthest, darkest corner in the cave and slept like a rock, before I had time to scare myself a little bit.

I don't know how long I had been asleep. But suddenly I sat up and was wide awake. I heard voices and I heard horses neighing outside my cave.

It was enough. A huge, wild terror swept over me again. Who knows, maybe the people talking out there were worse than any wolves?

"Drive the horses into the cave, so we have more room," I heard a voice say, and at once two horses strode in toward me. They neighed when they noticed Fyalar,

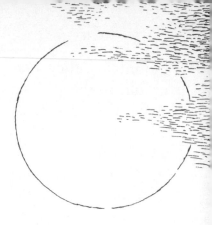

and Fyalar neighed back. Then they were quiet and they probably became friends in the darkness. No one in the glade outside must've realized that it was a strange horse they'd heard, because they continued talking calmly to each other.

Why had they come? Who were they? Why were they up here in the mountains at night? I must find out. I was so scared my teeth chattered and I wished I were a thousand miles away from here. But I was here and very close to me were some people who *could* be friends or just as easily be enemies, and I must find out which, no matter how frightened I still was. So I laid down flat on my stomach and began to crawl. Toward the voices out there. The moon was in the middle of the entrance to the cave, and a beam of moonlight fell right on my

hiding spot, but I kept myself in the darkness by the side and crawled slowly, slowly closer to the voices.

They sat out in the moonlight and were building a campfire, two men with rough faces and black helmets on their heads. It was the first time I'd seen some of Tengil's spies and soldiers, I knew what I was looking at, believe me! I knew that here were two of the cruel men who had joined up with Tengil to destroy Nangiyala's green valleys. I didn't want to fall into their hands, I'd rather have the wolves get me!

They talked secretively to each other, but in the darkness I was close to them and I heard every word. They certainly were angry at someone. Because one of them said:

"I'll slice his ears off, if he doesn't arrive on time this time too."

And then the other one said:

"Yes, he needs to learn. We sit here and wait in vain, night after night. What makes him so useful, really? Shooting doves which carry letters is fine, but Tengil wants more than that. He wants to have Sofia in Katla Cavern, and if this man can't arrange it, then it's a pity for him."

Then I understood which man they were talking about — and who they waited for — it was Hubert.

Calm down a little, I thought. Just wait until he's done skinning the wolf, then he'll come, believe me! He'll turn up on that path over there, the one who will catch Sofia for you!

Shame burned inside of me. I felt ashamed because we had a traitor in Cherry Valley. But I still wanted to see him come, yes, because now I would finally get proof. It was one thing to suspect someone, but now I would know for sure, so that I could say to Sofia:

"That Hubert, make sure you get rid of him! Otherwise it'll be the end of you and us and all of Cherry Valley!"

How terrifying it is to wait, when you're waiting for something so terrifying! A traitor is something terrifying, I felt it crawling within me as I laid there. I almost stopped being scared of the men by the campfire because of this strange feeling — that I'd see the traitor arrive soon on his horse, there on the path as it curved around the cliff. I dreaded it, yet I stared so that my eyes stung, toward the spot I knew he would appear.

The two by the campfire stared in the same direction. They also knew where he would come from. But none of us knew *when*.

We waited. They waited by their fire and I waited flat on my stomach in my cave. The moon had moved away from the entrance to the cave, but time certainly stood still. Nothing happened, we just waited! We waited until I wanted to jump up and shout to get it over with. It was as if everything waited, the moon and the mountains around us, the whole strange moonlit night held its breath and waited for the traitor.

And he came at last. Far away on the path, in the middle of the moonlight, a rider approached on his horse, yes, now I had him exactly where I knew he would appear. I shivered when I saw him — Hubert, I thought, how could you?

My eyes stung so that I had to close them. Or maybe I closed my eyes so that I wouldn't have to look. I had waited so long for this scoundrel, and now that he was actually coming, it was as if I couldn't bear to see his face. So I closed my eyes. And heard only from the plodding of horse's hooves, that he was approaching.

At last he arrived and reined in his horse. Then I opened my eyes. Because I needed to see what a traitor looked like, as he betrayed his own, yes, I wanted to see Hubert as he came to betray Cherry Valley and everyone who lived there.

But it wasn't Hubert. It was Jossi! The Golden Cockerel.

CHAPTER EIGHT

*J*OSSI! AND NONE OTHER!

It took me a moment to understand it. Jossi, he was so kind and happy and rosy-cheeked and he had given me cakes and comforted me when I was sad — he was the traitor.

And now he sat there by the fire just a little bit in front of me, together with Tengil's men — Veder and Kader he called them — explaining why he hadn't arrived earlier.

"Hubert was hunting wolves in the mountains last night, and I had to hide from him, you see."

Veder and Kader still looked sullen, and Jossi said even more.

87

"Hubert, surely you haven't forgotten him now? He should be in Katla Cavern just like Sofia should be, because he hates Tengil too."

"Then I think you should do something about it," said Veder.

"Because you're our man in Cherry Valley, isn't that right?" said Kader.

"Yes, of course, of course," said Jossi.

He fawned and tried flattery, but Veder and Kader didn't like him, I noticed. It must be true that no one likes a traitor, even if they have a use for him.

He got to keep his ears anyway, they didn't slice them off. But they did do something else, they put Katla's mark on him.

"All of Tengil's men must carry Katla's mark, even a traitor like you," said Veder. "So that you can show who you are, if any spies who don't know you go to Cherry Valley."

"Yes, of course, of course," said Jossi.

They ordered him to open his shirt and jacket, and with a branding iron warmed in the fire, they burned Katla's mark on his chest.

Jossi screamed when he felt the red-hot iron.

"Feel this," said Kader. "Now you'll know forever that you're one of us. Traitor that you are."

Of all the nights in my life, this one was surely the longest and the hardest, at least since I'd come to Nangiyala. And practically the worst thing was to lie there and listen to Jossi brag about his plans to destroy Cherry Valley.

Soon he would trap Sofia and Hubert, he said. Both of them.

"But it must take place so that no one realizes who lies behind it. How else could I continue to be Tengil's spy in Cherry Valley?"

You won't be a secret for long, I thought. Because I will expose you, so that you'll become pale, you red-faced scoundrel!

But then he said something else, Jossi, something that made my heart jump.

"Have you captured Jonathan Lionheart yet? Or is he still loose in Wild Rose Valley?"

Veder and Kader didn't like this question, I could see. "We're on his trail," said Veder. "A hundred men are searching for him day and night."

"And we'll find him even if we have to search every house in Wild Rose Valley," said Kader. "Tengil is waiting for him."

"I understand," said Jossi. "Young Lionheart is more dangerous than anyone else, I've told you that. Because he's truly a lion."

I felt proud, as I lay there, that Jonathan was such a lion. And what a relief it was to know that he was alive! But I cried with rage when I realized what Jossi had done. He had betrayed Jonathan. Only Jossi could have known about Jonathan's secret journey to Wild Rose Valley and sent a message about it to Tengil. It was Jossi's fault that one hundred men searched day and night for my brother and would hand him over to Tengil, if they found him.

But he lived, just think, he lived! And he was free too, so why had he called for help in my dream? As I lay there, I wondered if I'd ever know why.

I found out many other things, just by lying there and listening to Jossi.

"That Hubert, he's jealous of Sofia because we've chosen her as leader of Cherry Valley," said Jossi. "Well, it's because Hubert thinks he's the best at everything."

Oh, that's why! I remember how irritated Hubert sounded that time when he asked: "What's so special about Sofia?" Oh, it was because he was jealous, not because of anything else. Anyway, you could be jealous and still be a good man. But I had felt from the beginning that Hubert was Cherry Valley's traitor, and everything he said and did seemed to fit in with that. Just think how easily you could get the wrong idea about people! Poor Hubert, he had watched over me and saved my life and given me mutton and everything, and to think I had shouted at him: "Don't kill me!" No wonder he had been furious! Forgive me, Hubert, I thought, forgive me. I would remember to say that to him if I ever met him again.

Jossi was so sure of himself, he seemed quite smug as he sat there. But Katla's mark probably smarted, because he groaned a little every time Kader said:

"Feel that! Feel that!"

I wish that I could've seen what Katla's mark looked like. Though it was probably just terrible, I do believe, so it was a good thing to avoid.

Jossi continued to brag about everything he had done and everything he wanted to do, and right then he said:

"Lionheart has a little brother whom he loves more than anything else."

Then I cried silently and longed for Jonathan.

"That poor little one could definitely be used as bait to hook Sofia," said Jossi.

"You numbskull, why haven't you mentioned this little one before?" said Kader. "The brother, if we had him, could be used to force Lionheart out of his hideout. Because wherever he is, he would secretly find out that we've captured his brother."

"That would flush him out," said Veder. "Release my brother and take me instead, he'll say that if he really cares about his brother and wants to protect him from harm."

Now I was so scared that I couldn't even cry any more. But Jossi's head swelled and he boasted.

"I'll arrange it when I get back home," he said. "I can lure little Kalle Lionheart into a trap, it won't be difficult with a few cakes. Then we can deceive Sofia into coming to his rescue!"

"Isn't Sofia a little too clever for you?" said Kader. "Do you really think you can fool her?"

"Oh, yes, of course," said Jossi. "And she won't figure out who did it, because she trusts me."

Now he was pleased and chuckled to himself.

"Then you'll have both her and little Lionheart. How many white horses will Tengil give me for this, when he marches into Cherry Valley?"

We'll see about that, I thought. So, Jossi, you're going home to lure Kalle Lionheart into a trap! But if he isn't in Cherry Valley any longer, what'll you do then?

In the midst of all the misery, the thought of this made me a little happy! How disappointed Jossi would be when he found out that I had disappeared!

But then Jossi said:

"Little Kalle Lionheart, he's nice, but he definitely isn't a lion. There isn't a more easily frightened little coward. Cowardheart is the right name for him!"

Well, I knew that myself. That I could never be brave. And that I shouldn't really be called Lionheart like Jonathan! But it was still terrible to hear Jossi say it. I felt ashamed as I lay there, and I thought that I must, *must* try to be a little braver. But not right now, when I was so scared.

Jossi was finished at last. He didn't have any other evil deeds to boast about. And then he got up.

"I must be home, before dawn breaks," he said.

They urged him on until the last moment.

"Do something about Sofia and that little brother," said Veder.

"Trust me," said Jossi. "But don't harm the boy. I'm a little concerned about him."

Thanks, I've noticed that, I thought.

"And don't forget the password, if you come to Wild Rose Valley with information," said Kader. "If you want to be let in alive!"

"All power to Tengil, our liberator," said Jossi. "No, I'll remember that day and night. And Tengil, he won't forget his promise to me either, right?"

He already sat in the saddle, ready to go.

"Jossi, chief of Cherry Valley," he said. "Tengil has promised that's what I'll become, he hasn't forgotten?"

"Tengil forgets nothing," said Kader.

And so Jossi rode away. He disappeared the same

way he had come, and Veder and Kader sat there and watched him leave.

"That one," said Kader. "He'll be given to Katla, when we're done with Cherry Valley."

He said it so you realized, what it would be like to be under Katla's power. I knew so little about Katla, but I still shuddered and almost pitied Jossi, though he was such a coward.

The fire out in the glade had burned down. And I began to hope that Veder and Kader would also go away. I longed for them to disappear, so much that it ached. Like a rat sitting in a trap, I longed to be let go. If I could just get their horses out of the cave, before someone came in to get them, then I thought I could escape, and Veder and Kader would ride away without ever knowing how easily they could've caught Jonathan Lionheart's little brother.

But then I heard Kader say:

"We'll lie down in the cave and sleep for a while."

Oh, now it's all over, I thought. Yes, it's just as well, because I can't go on now. Let them take me, let it all be over!

But then Veder said:

"Why should we sleep? It'll be morning soon. And I have to get off this mountain. I want to go back to Wild Rose Valley now."

And Kader gave in to him.

"As you wish," he said. "Bring out the horses!"

Sometimes, when something is really dangerous, it's as if you save yourself without thinking. I threw myself backward and crawled into the cave's darkest corner, just like a small animal would've done. I saw Kader come toward the opening, but in the next instant he was inside the coal black cave and I couldn't see him any more. Just hear him, and that was terrible enough. He couldn't see me either, but he ought to have been able to hear my heart. How it beat, while I lay there and waited for what would come, when Veder found three horses instead of two.

They neighed a little, when Veder came in. All three, Fyalar too. I would know Fyalar's neigh among a thousand others. But Veder, the oaf, he couldn't hear the difference, he didn't notice that there were three horses in the cave. He drove out the two of them closest to the opening — their own — and he followed after them.

As soon as I was alone with Fyalar, I rushed over to him and put my hand on his nose. Please, please Fyalar, be quiet, I begged silently. Because I knew that if he neighed now, they would hear it outside and realize that something was wrong. And Fyalar, he was so smart. He understood everything. The other horses neighed outside. They wanted to say goodbye to him. But Fyalar stood quietly and didn't answer.

I saw Veder and Kader sitting up in their saddles, and I can't begin to describe how wonderful it felt. I'd soon be free now and out of this rattrap. I believed.

Then Veder said:

"I've forgotten my tinderbox."

And so he jumped off his horse again and began to look around the campfire.

Then he said:

"It isn't here. Maybe I dropped it inside the cave."

94

That's how the rattrap closed in on me again with a thunder and a crash, that's how I got caught. Veder came into the cave to search for that miserable tinder-box, and he walked straight into Fyalar.

I know you shouldn't lie, but if it's a matter of life or death, then you must.

He had strong hands, Veder, no one had ever held me so roughly before. It hurt and I became angry, almost more angry than scared, strangely enough. Maybe that's why I lied so well.

"How long have you been lying here spying?" roared Veder, as he dragged me out of the cave.

"Since last night," I said. "But I've just been sleeping," I said blinking in the morning light as if I'd just woken up.

"Sleeping," said Veder. "Are you saying that you didn't hear us bellowing and singing outside by the campfire? Don't lie now!"

He thought this was a cunning idea, because they hadn't sung a single note. But I was even more cunning.

"Well, maybe I heard a *little* when you were singing," I stammered, as if I were lying just to satisfy him.

Then Veder and Kader looked at each other, now they knew with complete certainty that I had been sleeping and hadn't heard a thing.

But that didn't help me any further.

"Don't you know that it's the death penalty for traveling this way?" said Veder.

I tried to appear as if I didn't know anything about the death penalty or anything else either.

"I only wanted to see the moonlight last night," I mumbled.

"And you risked your life for that, you little fox?" said Veder. "Where do you belong, in Cherry Valley or Wild Rose Valley?"

"In Wild Rose Valley," I said.

Because Karl Lionheart lived in Cherry Valley and I'd rather die then let them know who I was.

"Who are your parents?" asked Veder.

"I live with…with my grandfather," I said.

"What's his name then?" asked Veder.

"I just call him grandfather," I said, making myself look even more foolish.

"Where does he live in Wild Rose Valley?" asked Veder.

"In a…little white house," I said. Because I thought that houses in Wild Rose Valley would be white like they were in Cherry Valley.

"You'll show us this grandfather and this house," said Veder. "Get up on your horse!"

So we rode. And just then the sun rose over Nangiyala's mountains. The sky blazed like the reddest fire and the mountaintops glistened. Never in my life have I seen anything more beautiful or anything more grand. And if Kader and his horse's black rump weren't right in front of me, then I would've been jubilant, believe me. But I wasn't, no, I really wasn't!

The path continued to curve and twist exactly as before. But soon it dropped down steeply. I realized that we approached Wild Rose Valley. Yet I could hardly believe it, when I suddenly saw it right below me, oh, it was as beautiful as Cherry Valley, as it lay there in the morning light with its little houses and farms and its green slopes and flowering wild roses. There were entire drifts of wild roses. From up above it looked strange, almost like a sea with pink froth on the green waves, yes, Wild Rose Valley was the correct name for such a valley.

But I never would've reached the valley without Veder and Kader. Because there was a wall around all of Wild Rose Valley, a big wall that Tengil had forced the people there to build, since he wanted them imprisoned as slaves forever. Jonathan had told me that, that's how I knew.

Veder and Kader must have forgotten to ask me how I managed to sneak out of the enclosed valley, and I prayed to God that they wouldn't remember to either. Because what could I answer? How could a person go over the wall — and with a horse as well? Tengil's men, in black helmets and with swords and spears, stood watch up on the wall for as far as I could see. And likewise, a carefully guarded gate. Yes, there was a gate in the wall right where the path from Cherry Valley came to an end.

For many generations, people had traveled freely between the valleys. Now there was just one gate which was kept closed, and you had to be one of Tengil's men to go through.

Veder pounded on the gate with his sword. Then a little door opened and a gigantic man stuck his head out.

"Password," he shouted.

Veder and Kader whispered the secret password into

his ear. It was probably so that I wouldn't hear it. But that wasn't necessary, because I knew the words too — *All power to Tengil, our liberator!*

The man behind the door looked at me and said:

"And that one? Who's he?"

"He's a little fool we found up in the mountains," said Kader. "But he's not completely stupid because he managed to get past your gate last night, what do you say about that, Commander? I think you should ask your men how they conduct their watch at night."

The man behind the door became angry. He opened the gate. But he was yelling and swearing and didn't want to let me in, just Veder and Kader.

"Into Katla Cavern with him," he said. "He belongs there."

But Veder and Kader were persistent — I *would* go in, they said, because I must prove that I hadn't lied to them. It was their duty to Tengil to find out, they said.

And with Veder and Kader as escorts, I rode through the gate.

Then I thought that if I ever got to see Jonathan again, he would get to hear how Veder and Kader had helped me enter Wild Rose Valley. He would laugh about that for a long time.

But I didn't laugh. Because I knew how rotten things were for me. I had to find a white house with a grand-father inside, or else I'd go to Katla Cavern.

"Ride in front and show us the way," said Veder. "Because we need to have a serious talk with your grand-father now!"

I urged Fyalar along and turned onto a path that ran right along the wall.

There were plenty of white houses, just like at home in Cherry Valley. But I saw none that I dared to point out, because I didn't know who lived there. I didn't want to risk saying, "Grandfather lives there," because what if Veder and Kader strode in and there wasn't so much as one little old man? At least no one who wanted to be my grandfather.

Now I was really in a fix, and I was sweating as I rode. It had been so easy to lie about a grandfather, but now I thought that it wasn't such a good idea.

I saw people working outside their houses, but nowhere did I see anyone who resembled a grandfather, and I felt more and more miserable. It was also horrible to see how things were for the people of Wild Rose Valley, how pale and hungry and unhappy they all were, at least those that I saw along my ride, so different from the folks in Cherry Valley. But then we didn't have Tengil either, in our valley, treating us as his slaves and taking from us all that we lived on.

I rode and rode. Veder and Kader began to get impatient, but I just rode as if I were on the way to the ends of the earth.

"It is much farther?" asked Veder.

"No, not particularly," I said, but I didn't know what I was saying or doing. I was frightened out of my wits now and I was just waiting to be thrown into Katla Cavern.

But then a miracle happened. Believe it or not, outside a little white house next to the wall, an old man sat

on a bench feeding his doves. Maybe I wouldn't have dared to do what I did, if there hadn't been one that was snow-white among all the gray doves. Only one!

I got tears in my eyes, I had only seen doves like that with Sofia and one time at my window far away in another world.

And then I did something that was unheard of. I jumped off of Fyalar and with a few skips I was in front of the old man. I threw myself into his embrace and with my arms around his neck I whispered in despair:

"Help me! Save me! Say that you're my grandfather!"

I was so scared and sure that he would push me away, when he saw Veder and Kader in their black helmets behind me. Why would he lie for my sake and possibly end up in Katla Cavern for it?

But he didn't push me away. He held me and kept me in his embrace, and I felt his good, kind arms around me like a shield against all evil.

"Little boy," he said so loudly that Veder and Kader would hear, "Why have you been gone so long? And what have you done, unfortunate child, to come home with soldiers?"

My poor grandfather, what a lecture he got from Veder and Kader! They scolded and scolded and said that if he didn't take better care of his grandchildren and if he let them wander around Nangiyala's mountains, then soon he wouldn't have any grandchildren left, and they would see that he'd never forget it. But they would let it go this time, they said at last. And so they rode away. Soon their helmets appeared only as small black spots along the valley hillside below us.

102

Then I began to cry. I was still in my grandfather's arms and just cried and cried. Because the night had been so long and hard, and now it was finally over. And my grandfather, he held me. He just rocked me a little and I wished, oh, how I wished that he was my real grandfather, I tried to say that to him although I was crying.

"Yes, of course, I can be your grandfather," he said. "But just call me Mattias. What's your name?"

"Karl Lio…" I began. But then I kept silent. How could I be so crazy to say that name here in Wild Rose Valley?

"Dear grandfather, my name is a secret," I said. "Call me Scotty!"

"Yes, of course, Scotty," said Mattias and he laughed a little. "Go in the kitchen, Scotty, and wait for me there," he said then. "I'll just put your horse in the barn."

And I went in. Into a poor little kitchen with only a table and a wooden sofa and a chair and a fireplace. And a large sideboard by the wall.

Soon Mattias came back and then I said:

"We have a large sideboard like this one in our kitchen too, back home in Cherr…"

Then I went silent.

"Home in Cherry Valley," said Mattias, and I looked anxiously at him — once again I'd said something now that shouldn't have been mentioned.

But Mattias didn't say anything more. He went over to the window and looked out. He stood there for a while and searched as if he wanted to be sure that no one was nearby. Then he turned to me and said in a low voice:

"There is something special about the sideboard. Wait until you see!"

He placed his shoulder next to it and shoved the sideboard aside. Behind it there was a shutter in the wall. He opened it, and inside was a room, a very little room. Someone was lying there on the floor, sleeping.

It was Jonathan.

CHAPTER NINE

I CAN REMEMBER A FEW TIMES WHEN I'VE BEEN SO happy that I've scarcely known what to do. One time, when I was little and got a sled as a Christmas present from Jonathan, one that he had saved up to buy for a long time. And then the time when I first came to Nangiyala and found Jonathan down by the stream. And the whole first tremendous evening at Knights Farm, I was so joyfully happy then. But nothing, *nothing* else was like finding Jonathan on Mattias's floor, I never thought I could be so happy! It felt like a hearty laugh within my soul, because I was so happy now.

I didn't touch Jonathan. I didn't wake him. I didn't yell or feel jubilant. I just laid down next to him very quietly and fell asleep.

How long was I asleep? I don't know. The whole day, I believe. But when I awoke! Yes, when I awoke, Jonathan was sitting there on the floor beside me. He just sat there and smiled, no one could look as kind as Jonathan, when he smiles. I thought that he might not be happy that I'd come. That he might have already forgotten how he had called for help. But now I could see

105

that he was as glad as I was. So I had to smile with him and we sat there just looking at each other, saying nothing for a while.

"You cried for help," I said at last.

Then he stopped smiling.

"Why did you call?" I asked.

It was clearly something that he couldn't think about without getting upset. It was as if he hardly wanted to answer, he replied so quietly.

"I saw Katla," he said. "I saw what Katla does."

I didn't want to bother him with any questions about Katla, since I had so much to tell him, first and foremost about Jossi.

Jonathan could hardly believe it. His face turned white, he almost cried.

"Jossi, no, no, not Jossi," he said, getting tears in his eyes.

But then he got up.

"Sofia must find out immediately!"

"How will you do that?" I wondered.

"One of her doves is here," he said. "Bianca, she'll fly back tonight."

Sofia's dove, well, I couldn't believe it! I told Jonathan it was because of this dove that I was with him now and not in Katla Cavern.

"It's probably a miracle," I said, "that among all the houses in Wild Rose Valley that I came right to the one where you were. But if Bianca hadn't been sitting outside, then I would have ridden past."

"Bianca, Bianca, thank you for sitting there," said Jonathan. But he didn't have time to listen to me any longer, now he was in a hurry. He scratched his nails on the shutter, it sounded just like a little rat scratching. But it wasn't long before the door opened and Mattias peeked in.

"And little Scotty, he just sleeps and sleeps…" began Mattias, but Jonathan didn't let him continue.

"Fetch Bianca, if you'll be so kind," he said. "She must leave as soon as it starts to become dark."

He explained why. He talked with Mattias about Jossi. And Mattias shook his head as old people do, when they're sad.

"Jossi! Yes, I knew it must be someone from Cherry Valley," he said. "That's why Orvar is in Katla Cavern. My God, there are such people!"

Then he disappeared to get Bianca, and he closed the shutter to us.

It was a good hiding place Jonathan had here with Mattias. A little wooden room without windows or doors. The only way to go in and out was through the shutter behind the sideboard. No furniture was in it, just a cushion to sleep on. And a lamp that didn't light up the darkness much inside there.

In the light from the lamp Jonathan wrote a message to Sofia:

The traitor, cursed forever, his name is Jossi the Golden Cockerel. Get him quickly. My brother is here now.

"That's why Bianca flew here last night," said Jonathan. "To tell us that you had disappeared and were out looking for me."

"Just think, then Sofia understood the riddle I wrote on

107

the kitchen wall," I said. "When she came with the soup."

"What riddle?" said Jonathan.

"I'm searching for him far, far away beyond the mountains."

I told him what I had written. "It was so Sofia wouldn't be worried," I said.

Then Jonathan laughed.

"Not worried, yes, that's what you would think! And me? How calm do you think I felt when I found out you were somewhere up in Nangiyala's mountains?"

I must've looked ashamed, because he hurried to comfort me.

"Brave little Scotty, it was both lucky and fortunate that you were there! And even more lucky and fortunate that you are here now!"

That was the first time anyone had called me brave and I thought that if this kept up, then maybe I could be called Lionheart, without Jossi ruining it.

But then I remembered more that I had written on the wall at home. About one with a red beard who wanted white horses. And I asked Jonathan to add a line to the message:

It was wrong, what Karl said about red beard.

I also told him how Hubert had saved me from the wolves, and Jonathan said that he would be thankful to him for his whole life.

Twilight was falling over Wild Rose Valley as we released Bianca, and lights began shining everywhere, in the houses and farms on the hillside below us. It looked so calm and peaceful. And you could believe that people were sitting there now and eating their tasty evening meal or maybe they just talked with each other and played with their children and sang little tunes to them and things were fine and life was enjoyable. But you knew that it wasn't so. You knew that they hardly had anything to eat and that they weren't peaceful and happy at all, only unhappy. Tengil's men up on the wall with their swords and spears helped you remember how it was, in case you had forgotten.

A light did not burn in Mattias's window. His house was dark, and everything was quiet, as if there weren't a single living soul in it. But we were there, not inside the house but outside. Mattias stood watch by the corner of the house, and Jonathan and I crept among the wild rose bushes with Bianca.

These bushes were all around on of Mattias's farm. And wild roses are something that I like. Because they smell so good, not strong at all, just faintly. But I thought to myself that I would probably never again smell the fragrance of wild roses without my heart pounding and remembering how we crept among the wild rose bushes,

Jonathan and I. So close to the wall, where Tengil's men were listening and searching, perhaps most of all for one with the name of Lionheart.

Jonathan had darkened his face a little and pulled a hood down over his eyes. He didn't look like Jonathan, he didn't. But it was still risky and it could be a matter of life or death every time he left his hiding place in the secret room, he called it a hideout. A hundred men were searching for him day and night, which I knew and I had talked with him about it, but he just said:

"Yes, they'll probably carry on with the search."

He had to release Bianca himself, he said, because he wanted to be sure that no one saw her, as she flew away.

The guards along the wall each had their own section of the wall to patrol. A big one paced up and down the whole time on top of the wall behind Mattias's farm, we would have to be careful of him most of all.

But Mattias stood by the corner with a lantern, and he worked out how he would signal us. This is what he said:

"When I hold the lantern down low, then don't draw a single breath, because then Big Dodik is quite close. But when I hold the lantern high, then he is far away where the wall curves and he usually talks with one of Tengil's men there. Then you'll be able to release Bianca."

And we did.

"Fly, fly," said Jonathan, "fly, my Bianca, across Nangiyala's mountains to Cherry Valley. And watch out for Jossi's arrows!"

I don't really know if Sofia's doves understood human speech, but I almost believe that Bianca did. Because she laid her beak next to Jonathan's cheek as if she wanted to calm him, and then she flew off. She gleamed so white in the twilight, so dangerously white. How easily Big Dodik could've seen her, as she flew over the wall!

But he didn't. He probably stood there talking, and neither hearing nor seeing. Mattias kept watch and he didn't lower the lantern.

We saw Bianca disappear, and I pulled at Jonathan, now I wanted him to go back to the hideout quickly. But Jonathan didn't want to. Not yet. It was such a wonderful evening, the air was cool and so pleasant to breathe. He probably didn't feel like crawling into a stuffy little room. No one could understand this better than I, who had been confined so long to lying on my kitchen sofa back at home in town.

Jonathan was sitting in the grass with his arms around his knees and looking down at the valley. Quite calmly. You could almost believe he was thinking about sitting there the whole evening, despite all of Tengil's men who were walking along the wall behind him.

"Why are you sitting there?" I asked.

"Because I like it," said Jonathan. "Because I like this valley at dusk. And the cool air on my face, I like it too. And pink roses that smell of summer."

"I do too," I said.

"And I like the flowers and grass and trees and meadows and forests and pretty little lakes," said Jonathan. "And when the sun comes up and when the sun goes down and when the moon shines and the stars glisten and a few more things I can't remember right now."

"I like them too," I said.

"Everyone likes them," said Jonathan. "And if they don't ask for anything more, can you tell me then, why they can't have peace and quiet without someone like Tengil coming along and destroying everything?"

I couldn't answer and then Jonathan said:

"Come, it's best we go in!"

But we couldn't run right back in. First we had to know what was happening with Mattias and where Big Dodik was.

It had darkened. We couldn't see Mattias any longer, only the light from the lantern.

"He's holding it high, no Dodik there," said Jonathan. "Come now!"

But just as we began running, the light from the lantern dropped as quick as lightning, and we stopped. We heard galloping horses nearby and then they slowed down and someone talked to Mattias.

Jonathan gave me a little nudge in the back.

"Go," he whispered, "go to Mattias."

He threw himself right into a wild rose bush and I walked, scared and trembling, toward the lantern's light.

"I wanted to get a little air," I heard Mattias say. "It's such nice weather this evening."

"Nice weather," replied a gruff voice. "There's a death penalty for being out after sundown, didn't you know that?"

"A disobedient old grandfather, that's what you are," said another voice. "Where is your boy, by the way?"

"Here he comes," said Mattias, because I was getting close to him now. And I recognized the two on horseback. They were Veder and Kader.

"Aren't you going up in the mountains to look at the moonlight tonight?" said Veder. "What was your name, you little scamp? I never heard it."

"I'm just called Scotty," I said. I risked saying it because no one else knew that name, not Jossi or anyone, only Jonathan and Mattias and me.

"Scotty, really," said Kader. "Listen, Scotty, why do you think we've come here?"

Then it felt like my legs would buckle under me.

To put me into Katla Cavern, I thought. Naturally they regretted letting me go, and now they were coming to get me. What else could I believe?

"Well, you see," said Kader, "we ride around here in the valley during the evening to see that folks obey Tengil's orders. But your grandfather has a hard time understanding, maybe you can explain to him how bad it will be for both you and him, if you don't stay inside after it becomes dark."

"And don't forget," said Veder. "One more time and you won't escape, if we find you where you shouldn't be, remember that, Scotty! If your grandfather lives or dies, it makes no difference. But you're so young, you want to grow up and become one of Tengil's men, right?"

Tengil's man, no, I'd rather die, I thought, but I didn't say it. I was heartbroken over Jonathan and I couldn't risk irritating them, so I answered meekly:

"Yes, of course I want to."

"Fine," said Veder. "Then you can come down to the big pier tomorrow morning, so you'll be able to see Tengil, Wild Rose Valley's liberator. In the morning he's crossing the river of The Ancient Rivers in his golden sloop and coming ashore at the big pier."

Then they were ready to be off. But Kader reined in his horse at the last second.

"Listen, old man," he shouted to Mattias, who was already halfway into the house. "You haven't seen a handsome, light-haired youth called Lionheart, have you?"

I held Mattias by the hand, and I felt him shaking, but he answered calmly:

"I know no Lionheart."

"Really, you don't?" said Kader. "But if you were to accidentally chance upon meeting him, do you know what becomes of those who protect and hide him? The death penalty, you know that, right?"

Then Mattias shut the door behind us.

"The death penalty here and the death penalty there," he said. "That's all those people think about."

The sound of horses' hooves had scarcely died away, before Mattias was out with the lantern again. And soon Jonathan arrived, battered and scratched by thorns on his hands and face, but happy because nothing bad had happened and because Bianca was now in flight over the mountains.

We ate our evening meal later. There in the kitchen with Mattias. But with the shutter open so that Jonathan could quickly disappear into his hideout, if someone came.

But first we went out to the barn, Jonathan and I, and fed our horses. It was wonderful to see them together again. They stood with their heads so close to each other. I believe they were, in some way, telling each

other everything that had happened to them. I gave them oats, both of them. Jonathan wanted to stop me at first, but then he said:

"Yes, let them have it for once! But oats, you don't give them to *horses* any longer here in Wild Rose Valley."

When we went into the kitchen, Mattias had placed a bowl of soup on the table.

"We have nothing else, and it's mostly water," he said. "But at least it's warm."

I looked around for my knapsack, I remembered what I had inside it. And when I pulled out all of my loaves of bread and my mutton, they gasped, both Jonathan and Mattias, and their eyes began to shine. It felt so nice to lay out what was almost a feast to them. I cut up large slices of mutton, and we ate soup and bread and mutton, we ate and we ate! No one said anything, not for a long time. But at last Jonathan said:

"Oh, to have enough! I had almost forgotten how it felt to be full."

I became more and more pleased that I had come to Wild Rose Valley, it felt more and more right and good. And now I wanted to properly relate everything that had happened to me, from when I left home until Veder and Kader helped me into Wild Rose Valley. Much of it I had already talked about, but Jonathan wanted to hear it many times. Especially about Veder and Kader. He laughed at that, exactly like I thought he would. And Mattias too.

"They're not the most cunning, Tengil's men," said Mattias. "Although they think they are."

"No, even I could trick them," I said. "Think if they had known! The little brother they wanted so badly to catch, was the one they just helped into Wild Rose Valley and let go just like that."

When I said it, I began to wonder. I hadn't thought of it before, but now I asked:

"How in the world did you get into Wild Rose Valley, Jonathan?"

Jonathan laughed some more.

"I jumped in," he said.

"How did you jump…not with Grim?" I said.

"Yes," said Jonathan. "I don't have another horse."

I had seen them and I knew how well Jonathan could jump with Grim. But to fly over the wall around Wild Rose Valley, that was more than a person could believe.

"You see, the wall wasn't quite finished then," said Jonathan. "Not everywhere. Not to its full height. Though it was high enough, you can be sure of that."

"Yes, but the guards," I said. "Didn't they see you?"

Jonathan bit into his loaf of bread, then he laughed again.

"Yes, I had a whole swarm after me, and Grim took an arrow in his hind end. But I got away, and a kind-hearted farmer hid both me and Grim in his barn. And that night he lead me here to Mattias. Now you know everything."

"No, you don't know everything at all," said Mattias. "You don't know that people here in the valley sing songs about that ride and of Jonathan. That his coming here is the only happy thing that's happened in Wild Rose Valley, since Tengil invaded and made us slaves. 'Jonathan, our savior,' they sing, because they believe he will liberate Wild Rose Valley and I think so too. Now you know everything."

"You don't know everything at all," said Jonathan. "You don't know that Mattias is the leader of the secret rebellion in Wild Rose Valley, now that Orvar is in Katla Cavern. They should call Mattias the savior and not me."

"No, I'm too old," said Mattias. "He was right, Veder. If I live or die, it makes no difference."

"You shouldn't say that," I said. "Because you're my grandfather now."

"Yes, well then, for that reason I'll need to stay alive. But I'm not able to lead the fight any longer. You should be young for that."

He sighed.

"If only Orvar were still here! But he'll sit in Katla Cavern, until he's given to Katla."

Then I saw that Jonathan's face had become pale.

"Well, we'll see," he mumbled, "whom Katla gets in the end."

But then he said:

"Now we must get to work. You don't know either, Scotty, that here in this cottage we sleep during the day and work at night. Come, you'll see!"

He crawled in front of me through the shutter into the hideout, and there he showed me something. He threw aside the cushion that we had slept on, and pulled up a pair of wide floorboards under it, which were loose. Then I saw a black hole going right down into the ground.

"My underground passage begins here," said Jonathan.

"And where is the end?" I asked, although I almost guessed what he would answer.

"In the wild country on the other side of the wall," he said. "That's where it will end, once it's finished. Only a few more nights, then I think it will be long enough."

He crept down into the hole.

"But I must dig a bit more," he said. "Because, you see, I don't want to come up out of the dirt right under Big Dodik's nose."

Then he disappeared, and I sat there for a while and waited. When he finally came back, he pushed a wooden pail filled with dirt in front of himself. He heaved it up to me, and I hauled it out through the shutter to Mattias.

"More dirt for my field," said Mattias. "If I had a few peas and beans that I could sow and plant, there would be an end to the famine."

"Well, do you really believe that?" said Jonathan. "Out of ten beans from your field, Tengil takes nine, have you forgotten that?"

"You're right," said Mattias. "As long as Tengil exists, there will be hunger and need in Wild Rose Valley."

Now Mattias was going to sneak out and empty the pail in his field and I stood by the door and kept watch. I should whistle, Jonathan said, if I noticed the slightest thing that could be dangerous. I would whistle a special little melody that Jonathan had taught long ago, when we lived on Earth. We used to whistle together a lot, at that time. In the evenings when we went to bed. I've probably always been able to whistle.

Jonathan crawled back into his hole again to dig farther and Mattias closed the shutter and moved the sideboard.

"Get it into your head, Scotty," he said. "Never, never let Jonathan be inside without having the shutter closed and the sideboard in place in front of it. Get it into your head, that you're in a land where Tengil lives and rules."

"I won't forget," I said.

It was dark in the kitchen. Only a single candle burned on the table, but Mattias put it out.

"The night must be dark in Wild Rose Valley," he

said. "Because there are so many eyes that want to see what you don't want them to see."

Then he took the pail and disappeared, and I stood by the open door to keep watch. It was certainly dark like Mattias wanted. The houses were dark and the skies over Wild Rose Valley were dark. No stars were shining, and no moon, everything was black and I couldn't see anything at all. But all the eyes of the night, that Mattias talked about, they couldn't see anything either, I thought, and that was a comfort.

It felt depressing and lonely to stand there waiting, and a little eerie, too. Mattias took so long. I became worried, more and more worried with every moment that went by. Why didn't he come back? I stared into the darkness. But surely it wasn't as dark? Suddenly I realized that it had become lighter. Or was it just that my eyes had gotten used to it? Then I noticed it. The moon was breaking out through the clouds. It was the worst thing that could happen, and I prayed to God that Mattias would have time to get back, while there was still some darkness left to hide him. But then it was too late. Because the moon was shining in its full brilliance now, and a river of moonlight flowed over the valley.

In the light I saw Mattias. From a far distance, I saw him coming between the rose bushes with his pail. I looked around wildly, I should be keeping watch. And then I saw something else, too. Dodik, Big Dodik, with his back to me, came climbing down the wall on a rope ladder.

It's hard to whistle, when you're scared, so it didn't sound good. But I managed to get the melody out fair

120

enough. And quick as a lizard, Mattias vanished behind the closest rose bush.

By then Big Dodik was standing over me.

"What are you whistling for?" he roared.

"Because…because I learned how to today," I stammered. "I couldn't whistle before, but just think, suddenly I can today. Do you want to listen?"

I started again, but Dodik stopped me.

"No, be quiet," he said. "I don't know if it's forbidden to whistle, but I think it is. I don't think Tengil approves of it. And anyway, your door should be closed, do you understand?"

"Doesn't Tengil like it if your door is kept open?" I asked.

"That's not your concern," said Dodik. "Do as I say. But give me a ladle of water first. I'm dying of thirst, walking up there on the wall."

Then I thought quickly, if he followed me into the kitchen and didn't see Mattias there, what would happen then? Poor Mattias, the death penalty for those being out at night, I'd heard enough about that.

"I'll get it," I said hastily. "Stay here and I'll get the water for you."

I ran inside and I fumbled through the darkness toward the water barrel. I knew which corner it was in. I found the ladle, too, and I filled it with water. Then I felt that someone was standing behind me, yes, he was standing there in the darkness right behind my back, and I've never felt anything more creepy.

"Light a candle," said Dodik. "I want to see what this rattrap looks like."

My hands trembled, I trembled all over, but I still succeeded in lighting the candle.

Dodik took the ladle and drank. He drank and drank as if he were a bottomless pit. Then he threw the ladle on the floor and looked around suspiciously with his cruel little eyes. And he asked exactly what I expected he would ask.

"Where is old man Mattias, who lives here? Where is he?"

I didn't answer. I didn't know what I should say.

"Didn't you hear what I asked you?" he said. "Where is Mattias?"

"He's sleeping," I said. I had to make something up.

"Where?" said Dodik.

There is a little room next to the kitchen and I knew Mattias had his bed inside this room. But I also knew that he wasn't sleeping there now. Still I pointed to the door and said:

"Inside there!" I whined, so that it was scarcely heard. It sounded pitiful and Dodik laughed scornfully at me.

"You don't lie very well," he said. "Guess what we'll see next!"

He was so pleased, he knew that I lied, and he wanted to arrange the death sentence for Mattias and receive praise from Tengil. I knew it.

"Give me the candle," he said, and I gave it to him. I wanted to rush away from there, just dash out through the door and get Mattias and tell him to flee, before it was too late. But I couldn't move from my spot. I just stood there and felt sick, I was so scared.

Dodik saw this and he enjoyed it. He wasn't in a hurry, no, he smiled and dragged it out so that I would become even more scared. But when he was done smiling, he said:

"Come now, my boy, now you'll show me where old man Mattias is lying asleep."

He kicked open the door to the room and shoved me in, so that I stumbled over the threshold. Then he pulled me up again and stood in front of me with the candle in his hand.

"You liar, show me now," he said and held up the candle to brighten the dark room.

I didn't dare move or look up. I didn't want to be there, oh, it was hopeless!

But then, amidst my misery, I heard Mattias's angry voice:

"What are you staring at? Can't a person even sleep in peace at night?"

I looked up and saw Mattias, yes, he sat there in his bed back in the darkest corner of the small room, peering at the light. He was only wearing a shirt and his tousled hair looked as if he had been sleeping for a long time. In front of the open window, the pail stood next to the wall. Surely he was as quick as a lizard, the grandfather I had been given!

But I almost felt sorry for Dodik. Never have I seen anyone look so utterly dumbstruck, as he did, standing there glaring at Mattias.

"I only came to get a little water," he said sullenly.

"Water, yes, that's the trick," said Mattias. "Don't you know that Tengil has forbidden you to take water

123

from us? He believes that we'll poison you. If you come and wake me one more time, then I'll do it, too."

I don't understand how he dared to say that to Dodik. But maybe it was the right thing to say to one of Tengil's men. Because Dodik just grunted a little and left for his wall.

CHAPTER TEN

I HAD NEVER SEEN A TRULY CRUEL PERSON BEFORE I saw Tengil of Karmanyaka.

He came over the river of The Ancient Rivers in his golden sloop, and I stood there waiting with Mattias.

It was Jonathan who had sent me. He wanted me to see Tengil.

"Because then you'll understand better why folks here in the valley slave away and starve and die with only one thought and one dream — to see their valley free again."

High up in the mountains of The Ancient Mountains, Tengil had his castle. He lived there. He only crossed the river occasionally, to Wild Rose Valley, and he came to strike fear into the people, so that no one would forget who he was and begin to dream too much about freedom, said Jonathan.

At first I hardly saw anything. So many of Tengil's soldiers were standing there in front of me. Many long rows to protect Tengil, while he was in Wild Rose Valley. He had good reason, I think, to be scared that an arrow might coming whistling out from an ambush. Tyrants are always scared, Jonathan had said. And Tengil was the worst of all tyrants.

Well, at first we saw almost nothing, neither Mattias nor I. But then I found out what I could do. They stood there so self-assured and with their legs spread, Tengil's soldiers. If I lay flat on my stomach behind the one with his legs spread the farthest, I could peek through his legs.

But I couldn't get Mattias to do it.

"The main thing is that you watch," he said. "And that you never forget what you're seeing here today."

And I watched. A big, beautiful gilded ship approached us from out on the river, with black-clad men at the oars. There were many oars, more than I could count, and the oars' blades glittered in the sun every time they rose up over the water. The rowers worked hard. Strong currents pulled at the ship. Maybe the pull was from the waterfall farther down the river, because I heard the thunder of mighty waters far away.

"That's Karma Falls you hear," said Mattias, when I asked him. "The song of Karma Falls, it's our lullaby here in Wild Rose Valley, as the children lie in bed and listen, they fall asleep."

I thought about the children in Wild Rose Valley. Before, down here by the riverbank, they had run and played and splashed in the water and had fun. Now they couldn't. Because of the wall, the wall of hopelessness that enclosed everything. Along the whole wall there were only two gates, one that I had come through — it was called the main gate — and the other one here by the river, with the pier outside where Tengil's sloop now lay moored. The gate was open at this moment for Tengil and through the archway, between a soldier's legs,

I saw the pier and the black stallion that awaited Tengil, so fine with a saddle that glistened with gold and a bridle that glistened with gold. And I saw Tengil step forward and swing himself up into the saddle and go riding through the gate. Suddenly he was quite close to me, so that I could see his cruel face and his cruel eyes. Cruel as a serpent, Jonathan had said, and so he looked, bloodthirsty and cruel through and through. The clothes that he wore were as red as blood and the plumes in his helmet were red, as if he had dipped them in blood. And his eyes stared straight ahead, he didn't look at the people. It was as if there were nothing else in the world to him, nothing other than Tengil of Karmanyaka, yes, he was horrible!

Everyone in Wild Rose Valley had been commanded to come to the village square. Tengil would speak to them there. Mattias and I went, too, of course.

It was such a tidy and pretty little square with beautiful old houses surrounding it. Tengil had them there now, all the people of Wild Rose Valley, exactly as he had ordered. They stood quietly and just waited, but oh, how you could feel their bitterness and sorrow! Here on the square it had been pleasant before. They had probably danced here and played and sang on summer evenings or maybe they just sat on a bench outside the inn and talked with each other under the lindens.

Two old lindens grew there, and Tengil had ridden up and taken his spot between them. He stayed on horseback and stared out over the square and the people, but he didn't see any of them, I'm sure of it. He had his advisor next to him, a conceited one name Pjuke, I

found out from Mattias. Pjuke had a white horse almost as nice as Tengil's black one, and they sat there like two monarchs on their horses, just staring straight ahead. For a long time they sat like this. Around them the soldiers stood on guard, Tengil's men in black helmets and black cloaks and with their swords drawn. You could see they were sweating, because the sun was already high in the sky and it was a warm day.

"What do you think Tengil will say?" I asked Mattias.

"That he is dissatisfied with us," said Mattias. "He talks of nothing else."

Tengil didn't actually speak for himself. He would not talk to slaves. He only talked to Pjuke, and then Pjuke would announce how dissatisfied Tengil was with the folks in Wild Rose Valley. They worked poorly and sheltered Tengil's enemies.

"Lionheart has not been found yet," said Pjuke. "Our gracious sovereign is dissatisfied by this."

"Yes, I understand, I understand," I heard someone mumble right next to me. A poor wretch stood there, dressed in rags. A little old man with matted hair and a matted gray beard.

"Our gracious sovereign's patience will soon be at its end," said Pjuke, "and he has come to punish Wild Rose Valley harshly and without mercy."

"Yes, he's right, he's right," grumbled the old man next to me, and I realized that he must be a fool, and out of his mind.

"But," said Pjuke, "in his great goodness, our gracious sovereign will wait a while longer with his bloody punishment and he has even offered a reward. Twenty white horses go to the one who captures Lionheart for him."

"Then I'll get the fox," said the old man, and he pushed me in the side. "I'll get twenty white horses then, from our gracious sovereign, oh, that's good pay for such a little fox."

I became so angry that I wanted to hit him. Even if he was a fool, he shouldn't talk so stupidly.

"Have you no shame?" I whispered, and then he laughed.

"No, not much," he said. Then he looked right into my face and I saw his eyes. Only Jonathan had such beautiful shining eyes.

It was true, he really had no shame! How could he come here, right in front of Tengil's nose! Although no one recognized him, of course. Not even Mattias did. Not until Jonathan clapped him on the back and said:

"Old man, haven't we seen each other before?"

Jonathan liked to dress himself up. He used to act out parts for me in the kitchen in the evenings. When we lived on Earth, I mean. He could be very creepy and it was such fun. Sometimes I laughed so much that my stomach hurt.

But now, here, in front of Tengil, it was almost too brazen.

"I must see what's happening, too," he whispered, and now he wasn't laughing. There was nothing to laugh at either.

Because Tengil had all the men of Wild Rose Valley stand in line in front of him, and with his cruel forefinger, he pointed out those who would be taken across the river to Karmanyaka. I knew what that meant, Jonathan had told me. None of the ones whom Tengil pointed to would come back alive. They would be slaves in Karmanyaka and drag stones up to the fortress Tengil was having built on the highest mountain in The Ancient Mountains. It would be a fortress that could never be captured by an enemy, and Tengil would sit there in all his cruelty, year in and year out, finally feeling safe. But many slaves were needed to build such a fortress, and the slaves worked until they dropped.

"And then Katla gets them," Jonathan had said. When I remembered that I shivered in the warmth of the sun. Katla was still just an awful name to me then, nothing more.

It was quiet on the square, when Tengil pointed. Only a little bird sat high up in the tree above him, singing and trilling so beautifully. The bird probably didn't know what Tengil was doing down there under the linden trees.

But there was crying, too. It was pitiful to hear them cry, all the women who would lose their men and all the children who would never see their fathers again. Everyone cried, I did too.

Tengil, he didn't hear the crying. He sat on his horse and pointed and pointed, and the diamond on his forefinger flashed every time he ordered someone to death. It was terrible, he ordered folks to death with just his forefinger!

But one of them he pointed to must've gone crazy, when he heard his children crying. Because suddenly he broke out of line, and before the soldiers could stop him, he rushed toward Tengil.

132

"Tyrant," he shrieked. "One day you will die, too, have you thought of that!"

And then he spat on Tengil.

Tengil's expression didn't change. He just made a sign with his hand, and the soldier standing the closest raised his sword. I saw how it glittered in the sunshine, but at that same moment Jonathan grasped me by the neck and pressed me to his chest, he hid my face, so that I saw nothing more. But I felt, or maybe I heard, the sobbing in Jonathan's chest. And when we went home he cried. Something he never used to do.

They mourned in Wild Rose Valley that day. Everyone mourned. Everyone except Tengil's soldiers. On the contrary, they were happy each time Tengil came to Wild Rose Valley, because he threw a feast for his men. The poor man's blood had hardly dried, the one who was killed on the square, when a large keg of beer was brought out and pigs were roasted whole on the spit, so that the smell lay thick over Wild Rose Valley and all of Tengil's men ate and drank and bragged about Tengil, who gave them so many good things.

"But they take Wild Rose Valley's pigs, the thieves," said Mattias, "and it's Wild Rose Valley's beer that they drink."

Tengil was not at the feast. When he was done pointing, he went back across the river.

"And now he is probably sitting contentedly in his castle and believes that he has struck terror into Wild Rose Valley," said Jonathan, when we got home. "He probably thinks we are just frightened slaves and nothing else."

"But he's wrong," said Mattias. "What Tengil doesn't

133

understand, is that he can never suppress people who fight for their freedom and stay together as we do."

We went past a little house with apple trees around it, and Mattias said:

"That's where he lived, the one who was just killed."

On the stones steps outside, a woman was sitting. I recognized her from the square, I remember how she screamed, when Tengil pointed to her man. Now she sat with scissors in her hand, busily cutting off her long, fair hair.

"What are you doing, Antonia?" asked Mattias. "What will you do with your hair?"

"Bowstrings," said Antonia.

She didn't say anything more. But I shall never forget how her eyes looked, when she said that.

Many things brought the death penalty in Wild Rose Valley, Jonathan had said. But it was most risky to have weapons, it was forbidden more than anything else. Tengil's soldiers went around searching in homes and farms, looking for hidden bows and arrows and hidden swords and spears. But they never found anything. Yet there wasn't a single house or farm that didn't have weapons hidden, and weapons forged for the battle that must come in the end, said Jonathan.

Tengil had also promised white horses as a reward, to those who exposed hidden weapons.

"How foolish," said Mattias. "Does he really think there is a single traitor in Wild Rose Valley!"

"No, it's just Cherry Valley that has one," said Jonathan sadly. Well, I knew that it was Jonathan walking next to me, but it was hard to remember, with the way he looked in his beard and his rags.

"Jossi hasn't seen the atrocities and oppression we have seen," said Mattias. "Or else he could never do what he is doing."

"I wonder what Sofia is doing?" said Jonathan. "And I really want to know if Bianca got there alive."

"We sincerely hope that she did," said Mattias. "And that Sofia has now put a stop to Jossi."

When we arrived home at Mattias's farm, we saw Big Dodik lying in the green grass and playing dice with three more of Tengil's men. They had a day off, I think, because they laid there among the rose bushes the whole afternoon, we could see them from the kitchen window. They played dice and ate pork and drank beer, that they had gotten at the square, several full pitchers. Gradually they stopped playing dice. Then they ate pork and drank beer. Then they just drank beer. Then they did nothing, they just crawled around like beetles in the bushes. At last they fell asleep, all four of them.

Their helmets and cloaks lay in the grass, they had thrown them off. No one could drink beer in a thick woolen cloak on such a warm day.

"But if Tengil knew, he would have them flogged," said Jonathan.

Then he disappeared out through the door, and before I even had time to be scared, he was back with a cloak and a helmet.

"What do you have those awful things for?" asked Mattias.

"I don't know yet," said Jonathan. "But there may come a time when I need them."

"There may come a time when you'll slip up, too," said Mattias.

But Jonathan ripped off his rags and his beard and put on his helmet and cloak, and he stood there looking exactly like one of Tengil's men, it was terrible. Mattias trembled and begged him for God's sake to hide those awful things inside the hideout.

And Jonathan did.

Then we lay down and slept the rest of the day, so that's why I don't know what happened when Big Dodik and his companions woke up and tried to figure out whose helmet and cloak were gone.

Mattias slept too, but he woke for a moment, he said afterward, and heard shouting and cursing from out in the rose bushes.

That night we worked farther on the underground passage.

"Three more nights, no longer," said Jonathan.

"And what will happen then?" I asked.

"What I've come here to do, will happen," said Jonathan. "Maybe it won't succeed, but I must try. To free Orvar."

"Not without me," I said. "You won't leave without me again. Wherever you go, I'm going too."

Then he looked at me for a long time, and then he smiled.

"All right, if you really want to, then that's also what I want," he said.

CHAPTER ELEVEN

*A*LL OF TENGIL'S SOLDIERS WERE INVIGORATED FROM so much pork and beer, and all of them definitely wanted twenty white horses. Because now they were searching desperately for Jonathan. They immediately began searching from morning to night, prying in every corner of every house in the valley. Jonathan kept himself in the hideout until he almost suffocated.

And Veder and Kader rode around everywhere, reading a proclamation out loud about my brother. I had the chance, one time, to hear it, too, about "Tengil's enemy, Jonathan Lionheart, who has gone over the wall without permission and whose whereabouts in Wild Rose Valley are still unknown." They described what he looked like. He was "a remarkably handsome, slender youth with light hair and dark blue eyes," they said and I think that Jossi had described him well. And we heard about the death penalty again for those who sheltered Lionheart and the reward one would receive for betraying him.

While Veder and Kader rode around bellowing about this, people came to Mattias's farm to say farewell to Jonathan and to thank him for everything he had done for them, which was probably much more than I knew about.

"We'll never forget you," they said with tears in their eyes, and they brought bread and gave it to him, though they hardly had anything to eat.

"You'll need it, because it's a difficult and dangerous journey you're embarking on," they said, and then they hurried away to have time to hear Veder and Kader once more. Just for fun.

The soldiers came to Mattias's farm too. I sat on a stool in the kitchen, horrified as they strode about, and dared not move. But Mattias was arrogant.

"What are you looking for?" he said. "That Lionheart, I don't think he exists. He's just something you made up so that you can go around and mess up folks' homes."

The certainly did mess it up. They began inside the little room. They threw all of the bedclothes onto the floor. Then they rummaged through a chest standing in there, they heaved everything out of it, which was pretty silly. Did they really think that Jonathan was hiding in the chest?

"Why don't you look in the kitchen cabinets?" asked Mattias. But then they became angry.

And they went into the kitchen and started working on the sideboard, and I sat there on my stool and felt hatred rising up inside me. This was the night we would leave the valley, Jonathan and I, and I thought that if they found him now, I wouldn't know what to do! Fate *couldn't* be so cruel, that they would get Jonathan during his final hours in Wild Rose Valley.

Mattias had stuffed the sideboard with old clothes and sheep's wool and things to reduce the sound coming from inside the hideout, and they had heaved all that junk out onto the kitchen floor.

And then! Then I wanted to scream, to make the house collapse, yes, because one of them put his shoulder against the sideboard to push it aside. But no cries came from me. I sat like a stone on my stool and just hated him, everything about him, his rough hands and thick neck and the wart on his forehead! I hated him, because now I knew that he was going to see the shutter to the hideout, and that meant the end for Jonathan.

But there came a cry. From Mattias.

"Look, fire!" he shouted. "Has Tengil said you should set our houses on fire?"

I don't know how it started, but it was true. The sheep's wool burned briskly on the floor, and the soldiers hurried to put it out. They jumped and stomped and swore noisily, and at last they turned the water barrel over. So the fire was put out almost before it had begun. But Mattias was still angry and scolded them.

"Don't you have any sense in your head?" he said. "You can't toss wool on the floor right next to the fire, where it smolders and sparks."

The one with the wart was furious.

"Silence, old man," he said. "Or else I know of several good ways to shut that mouth of yours!"

But Mattias didn't allow himself to be scared.

"You will clean up after yourselves," he said. "Look around here! It's like a pigsty."

That was the right way to get them to leave.

"Clean up your pigsty yourself, old man," said the one with the wart and he marched out first. The others followed. And the door was left wide open behind them.

"They have no sense," said Mattias.

"What luck that it started to burn," I said. "How lucky for Jonathan!"

Mattias blew on his fingertips.

"Yes, small fires can be good sometimes, accidentally," he said. "Though you burn yourself, when you throw glowing coals out of the fireplace using your hands."

But our sorrows were still not over, whatever I'd believed.

They looked for Jonathan in the barn too, and afterward the one with the wart went to Mattias and said:

"You have two horses, old man! No one in Wild Rose Valley is allowed more than one, you know that! We're sending a man here, from the other side, tonight. He'll take the one with the white blaze, you're giving it to Tengil."

"But it's the boy's horse," said Mattias.

"Really! Well it's Tengil's now, anyway."

That's what he said, the soldier. And I began to cry. Tonight we were to leave Wild Rose Valley, Jonathan and I. Our long underground passage was done. And not until now had I thought about it — how in all the world could we take Grim and Fyalar with us? They couldn't crawl through the underground passage. What a nut I was to not have understood it before! That we must leave our horses with Mattias. And wasn't that sad enough? But why must it be even more awful? Tengil would have Fyalar, it broke my heart in two when I heard it!

The one with the wart pulled a little wooden tag out of his pocket and held it under Mattias's nose.

"Here," he said. "Write your property mark here!"

"Why should I do that?" asked Mattias.

"Well, it means that you're joyfully giving this horse to Tengil."

"I don't feel joyful," said Mattias.

But then the soldier went up close to him, with a drawn sword.

"You certainly do," he said. "You feel very joyful and this is where you put your mark! And you'll give this tag to the man who comes over from Karmanyaka to take the horse. Because Tengil wants proof that you give of your own free will, do you understand, old man?" he said and shoved Mattias so that he almost fell down.

What could Mattias do? He wrote down his property mark, and the soldiers disappeared from Mattias's farm to look for Jonathan in other places.

It was our last evening with Mattias. We sat at his table for the last time and for the last time he offered us soup. We were sad, all three. I was most of all. I cried. For Fyalar's sake. And for Mattias's sake. He had almost become my grandfather, and now I was leaving him. I cried, too, because I was so little and scared and I couldn't do anything at all, when the soldiers came and shoved my grandfather.

Jonathan sat quietly thinking, and suddenly he mumbled:

"If only I knew the password!"

"What password?" I asked.

"You must give the password, when you go in or out through the main gate, didn't you know?" he said.

"Yes, I know that," I said. "And I also know the

password — *'All power to Tengil, our liberator,'* I heard it from Jossi, didn't I tell you?"

Jonathan looked at me. He stared at me for a long time, and then he began to laugh.

"Scotty, I like you," he said. "Did you know that?"

I didn't understand why he was so happy about the password, because he wouldn't be going through the main gate, anyway. But I was a little happy too, amidst all this sorrow, that I could cheer him up with such a little thing.

Mattias had gone into the room to clean up, and Jonathan rushed in after him. They talked in low voices to each other in there. I didn't hear much, just that Jonathan said:

"If I fail, then you'll take good care of my brother?"

Then he came back to me.

"Listen now, Scotty," he said. "I'm taking the pack and leaving first. And you'll wait here with Mattias, until you hear from me again. It may take a long time, because I have a few things I must do first."

Oh, I didn't like that! I've never been able to stand waiting for Jonathan. Especially when I'm scared at the same time, and I was scared now. Because who knows what Jonathan would meet, out on the other side of the wall? And what was he thinking of doing that might fail?

"You shouldn't be so scared, Scotty," said Jonathan. "You are Karl Lionheart nowadays, don't forget it!"

Then he said a hasty goodbye to Mattias and me and crept inside the hideout. And we saw him disappear down into his underground passage. He waved, the last thing we saw was his hand waving to us.

And then we were left alone, Mattias and I.

"Big Dodik doesn't know a mole is creeping underneath his wall right now," said Mattias.

"No, but what if he notices when the moles sticks its head up out of the ground," I said. "And then throws his spear!"

I was so sad and I slipped out to the barn to see Fyalar. One last time I sought him out for comfort. But he couldn't comfort me, when I knew that after tonight I would never see him again.

It was dark in the barn. The window was small and didn't let in much light, but I saw how eagerly Fyalar turned his head, when I came through the door. I went to him in his stall and threw my arms around his neck. I wished he could understand, that it wasn't my fault, what must happen.

"Though perhaps it is my fault," I said and cried. "If I had stayed in Cherry Valley, then Tengil would never get you! Forgive me, Fyalar, forgive me! But I couldn't do anything else."

I think he understood that I was sad. He put his soft muzzle against my ear. It was as if he didn't want me to cry.

But I cried. I stood there with him and cried and cried, until I didn't have any tears left. Then I groomed him and gave him the last of the oats, well, he split them with Grim, of course.

I had such terrible thoughts, while I groomed Fyalar.

May he drop dead, the man who comes to take my horse, I thought. May he die before he crosses over the river! It was a terrible thing to wish, it really was. And it didn't help.

No, he was probably on the ferry already, I thought, the ferry that they carry all their stolen goods with. Maybe he's already landed. Maybe he's coming through the main gate right now, and he'll be here soon. Oh, Fyalar, if only we could run away somewhere together, you and I!

Just as I thought that, someone opened the barn door, and I screamed, I was so scared. But it was just Mattias. He had begun to wonder what was taking me so long. I was glad that it was dark inside the barn. He

wouldn't see that I had been crying again. But he understood, because he said:

"Little guy, if only I could do something! But a
grandfather can't help with this. So just cry."

Then I looked through the window behind him,
someone out there was approaching Mattias's farm. One
of Tengil's men! The one who would take Fyalar away!

"Here he comes!" I screamed. "Mattias, he's coming
now!"

Fyalar neighed. He didn't like me shouting so hope-
lessly.

The next moment the barn door was pulled open,
and he stood there in his black helmet and black cloak.

"No," I screamed, "no, no!"

But then he was already next to me and flung his
arms around me.

Jonathan did! Because it was him!

"Don't you recognize your own brother?" he said,
when I struggled against him. He pulled me to the window so that I could see him better. Still I could hardly
believe it was Jonathan. He wasn't recognizable.
Because he was so ugly. Uglier than me, even, and not
a 'remarkably handsome youth' at all. His hair hung in
soggy strips around him, not shining like gold, and he
had put some kind of strange snuff under his top lip. I
didn't know that you could become so ugly with so little. He looked stupid. I would've laughed, if there had
been time. But Jonathan clearly didn't have time for
anything.

"Quick, quick," he said, "I must leave immediately.
The one from Karmanyaka will be here any minute!"

He stuck his hand out toward Mattias.

"Bring the tag here," he said. "Because I'm sure you're giving both of your horses to Tengil, joyfully?"

"Well, what do you think?" said Mattias as he pressed the tag into his hand.

Jonathan put it in his pocket.

"I'll show this at the gate," he said. "Then the commander will see I'm not lying."

It all happened so quickly. We saddled the horses faster than ever before. And during that time Jonathan talked about how he came through the main gate. Because Mattias wanted to hear.

"It was easy," said Jonathan. "I gave the password exactly like Scotty taught me — *All power to Tengil, our liberator* — then the commander said: 'Where are you from, where are you going and what is your task?' 'From Karmanyaka to Mattias's farm to get two horses for Tengil,' I said. 'Pass,' he said. 'Thanks,' I said. And now here I am. But I must go out through the gate, before the next man of Tengil's comes and wants in, otherwise it will become difficult."

We brought the horses out of the barn faster than I can say, and Jonathan swung himself up in the saddle on Grim. He held Fyalar's reins next to him.

"Take care of yourself, Mattias," he said. "Until we meet again!"

And so he trotted away, with both horses. Just like that!

"Well, but what about me," I cried. "What should I do?"

Jonathan waved to me.

"You'll find out from Mattias," he shouted.

And I stood there and stared after him and felt foolish. But Mattias explained it to me.

"You understand that *you* could never slip through the main gate," he said. "You have to crawl through the passage, as soon as it becomes dark. Then Jonathan will be there on the other side, waiting for you."

"Are you sure?" I said. "Something could happen to him at the last minute."

Mattias sighed.

"Nothing is certain in a world where there is Tengil," he said. "But if things go wrong, then you come back and stay here with me."

I tried to think of what it would be like. At first crawling along the passage completely alone. That was terrible, just that part. And to come up in the forest on the other side of the wall and not find Jonathan there at all. And sitting there in the darkness and waiting and waiting and realizing at last, that everything had gone wrong. And then crawling back again. And living without Jonathan!

We stood in front of the barn which was now empty. And then suddenly I thought of something else, too.

"What will happen to you, Mattias, when he comes, the man from Karmanyaka, and there's not a horse in the barn?"

"Well, of course there'll be a horse," said Mattias. "Because I have to hurry now and bring my own home. I've been boarding it at a neighbor's farm, while Grim stayed in my barn."

"Yes, but then he'll take your horse instead," I said.

"He'd better try!" said Mattias.

At the last minute Mattias brought his horse home. For just after he arrived, the man came to take Fyalar. At first he screamed and shouted and swore like all the rest of Tengil's men. Because there was only one horse in the barn and because Mattias wouldn't hand him over.

"Don't try," said Mattias. "You know we're allowed to have *one* horse. And you've already taken the other one, for God's sake, the one with my mark on it. I can't help it if you've made a mess of it all, that one blockhead doesn't know what the other one does."

Some of Tengil's men became angry, when Mattias acted superior to them, but some of them became docile and meek, and the one who came for Fyalar, he gave up completely.

"Something must be wrong then," he said and he slipped away toward the path like a dog with its tail between its legs.

"Mattias, are you ever scared?" I asked, when the man wasn't visible any longer.

"Yes, of course, I'm scared," said Mattias. "Feel how my heart is pounding," he said, and he took my hand and laid it on his chest. "We are all scared," he said. "But sometimes you can't show it."

Then evening came and darkness. And it was time for me to leave Wild Rose Valley. And Mattias.

"Goodbye, little guy," said Mattias. "Don't forget your grandfather!"

"No, never, I will never forget you," I said.

And I was alone underground. I crept through the long, dark tunnel, and I talked to myself the whole time because it helped keep me calm and to not get scared.

"No, it *doesn't* matter that it's pitch black...no, you *certainly* won't suffocate...yes, a little dirt is dropping down your neck, but it *doesn't* mean the whole tunnel will collapse, you fool! No, no, Dodik *won't* see you, when you climb out, he's not a cat that can see in the dark! Of course, Jonathan will *definitely* be there waiting for you, he *is* there, do you hear what I'm saying? He *is!* He *is!*"

And he was. He sat on a stone, in the darkness, and a little way from him Grim and Fyalar stood under a tree.

"Well, Karl Lionheart," he said, "you're here at last!"

CHAPTER TWELVE

WE SLEPT UNDER A SPRUCE THAT NIGHT, AND WE woke early at dawn. And froze. At least I did. A mist was lying between the trees, we could hardly see Grim and Fyalar. They looked like gray phantom horses in all the dreariness and silence around us. It was completely silent. And melancholy in some way. I don't know why things seemed so melancholy and desolate and frightening, waking up that morning. I just knew that I longed to be back in the warm kitchen with Mattias and dreaded what awaited us. All the things which I didn't know anything about.

I tried not to show Jonathan how I felt. Because who knows, he might send me back, and I *wanted* to be with him through every danger, however risky it was.

Jonathan looked at me and smiled a little.

"Don't look like that, Scotty," he said. "This is nothing. It'll probably get worse!"

151

Well, that was comforting! But just then the bright sun came out and the mist vanished. The birds began to sing in the forest, all the gloom and desolation flew away at the same time, and it didn't feel so dangerous any more. I warmed up, too. The sunshine was nice and warm already. Everything felt better, it almost felt good.

Grim and Fyalar felt good, too. They had escaped from their dark stalls and could now graze on soft, green grass again. They liked it, I think.

Jonathan whistled to them, a quiet little whistle, but they heard it and came.

Jonathan wanted to go away now. Far away! At once!

"Because the wall is just behind that hazel thicket," he said. "And I don't feel like coming face to face with Dodik."

Our underground passage came up between a pair of hazelnut bushes. But the opening was no longer visible, Jonathan had covered it with twigs and branches. He marked the place with a pair of sticks, so that we could find the tunnel again.

"Don't forget what it looks like here," he said. "Remember that large stone and the spruce where we slept and the hazel thicket. Because there may come a time when we'll be this way again. If not..."

Then he went silent and said no more. And we mounted our horses and rode quietly away from there.

Then a dove came flying over the treetops. One of Sofia's white doves.

"There's Paloma," said Jonathan. I don't know how he could recognize her from so far away.

We had waited a long time to hear from Sofia. And

now at last her dove arrived, when we were already outside the wall. She flew right to Mattias's farm. Soon she
would fly down into her loft outside the barn, but only
Mattias would be there to read her message.

It worried Jonathan.

"Couldn't the dove have come yesterday?" he said.
"So that I could've learned what I need to know."

But we must go on now, go far away from Wild Rose
Valley and the wall and all of Tengil's men that hunted
Jonathan.

We would make our way to the river, taking a detour
through the forest, said Jonathan, and then follow the
banks to Karma Falls.

"And there little Karl, there you will see a waterfall
like you've never dreamed of!"

"No, I've never dreamed of one," I said. "I've never
seen a mighty waterfall."

There really wasn't much I had seen, before I came
to Nangiyala. Not even a forest, as we rode through now.
It was truly like a forest from a saga, dark and dense, and
there were no cleared trails. We rode right through the
trees, which slapped their wet branches against our faces.
But I still liked it. Everything — seeing the sunlight
flowing through the tree trunks and hearing the birds
and the smell of wet trees and wet grass and horses. And
most of all, I liked riding there with Jonathan.

The air was brisk and cool in the forest, but as we
rode, it became warmer. We would have a hot day, we
felt it already.

Soon Wild Rose Valley was far behind us and we
were deep within the forest. And there in a glade, with

tall trees around it, we found a small gray cottage. In the middle of a dark forest, how could anyone live in such a lonely place! But someone lived there. Smoke came out of the chimney and a pair of goats grazed outside.

"Elfrida lives here," said Jonathan. "She'll probably give us a little goat milk, if we ask her."

And we got milk, as much as we wanted to have, which was good, because we had ridden far and had not eaten anything. We sat on Elfrida's stone steps and drank her goat milk and ate bread that we had with us in our pack and goat cheese that Elfrida gave us and a handful of wild strawberries I had picked in the forest. It all tasted good together, and our hunger was satisfied.

Elfrida, she was a plump little, kindly old woman, and she lived alone there, with just her goats and a gray cat for company.

"Praise God, I don't live within any walls," she said.

She knew many people in Wild Rose Valley and she wanted to know if they still lived. Jonathan told her. He was sad when he did, because most of it was news that a kind old person must grieve to hear.

"That things would be so awful in Wild Rose Valley," said Elfrida. "A curse on Tengil! And on Katla! Everything would be fine, if only he didn't have Katla!"

She threw her apron over her eyes, I think she was crying.

I couldn't stand to watch this, so I went to search for more wild strawberries. But Jonathan stayed and talked longer to Elfrida.

I pondered while I picked my wild strawberries. Who was Katla and where was Katla? When would I find out?

We reached the river little by little. It was during the hottest time of the day, at noon. The sun was sitting like a ball of fire up in the sky and it glittered on the water too, shining like a thousand small suns. We stood high up on the hillside and saw the river far below us. What a sight it was! The river of The Ancient Rivers rushed toward Karma Falls, frothing and whirling, the mighty waters wanted to go there and we could hear the falls far away.

We wanted to go down to the water and cool off. Grim and Fyalar were turned loose in the forest and they found a stream where they could drink. But we wanted to swim in the river. So we rushed down the steep hillside and tore our clothes off while we ran. Willow trees grew down at the river's edge. One willow stretched its trunk far out over the river and trailed its branches in the water. We climbed out on the trunk and Jonathan showed me how to cling to a branch and lower myself down into the whirling water.

"But don't lose your grip," he said, "because then you'll go to Karma Falls faster than is good for you."

And I held tight so that my knuckles whitened. I swung there on my branch and let the water spill over me. Never have I had such a wonderful dip and never one as dangerous either. I felt the pull of Karma Falls through my whole body.

Then I climbed up on the trunk again, Jonathan helped me and we sat in the top of the willow tree, as if in a green house rocking over the water. The river skipped and played right under us. It wanted to entice us down again, to try and make us think it wasn't dangerous at all. But I only needed to dip my toes in and with just my big toe, I could feel the pull that wanted to drag me in.

As I was sitting there, I happened to glance up at the hillside, and then I became scared. Riders were up there, Tengil's soldiers with long spears. They came galloping, but because of the roaring water we hadn't heard the sound of horses' hooves.

Jonathan saw them too, but I didn't notice him growing scared. We sat there silently and waited for them to ride past. But they didn't ride past. They stopped, they jumped off of their horses, as if they were thinking about resting, or something like that.

I asked Jonathan:

"Do you think they're after you?"

"No," said Jonathan. "They're going from Karmanyaka to Wild Rose Valley. There's a rope bridge suspended across the river by Karma Falls, Tengil usually sends most of his soldiers that way."

"But they didn't have to stop right here," I said.

Jonathan agreed with that.

"I really don't want them to see me," he said, "and get any ideas about Lionhearts in their heads."

Six of them, I counted up on the slope. They talked noisily about something and pointed to the water, though we couldn't hear what they were saying. But suddenly one of them started driving his horse down the hillside, down to the river. He came riding almost straight at us, and I was glad that we were sitting so well hidden in the tree.

The others shouted to him:

"Don't do it, Park! You'll drown both yourself and your horse!"

But he — the one they called Park — just laughed and shouted back:

"I'll show you! If I don't make it to that rock and back, then a round of beer is on me, I swear!"

Then we realized what he wanted to do.

Part of a rock was jutting out of the river. The current broke around it and only a bit of it was above the surface. But Park had happened to see it, as they rode past and now he wanted to show off.

"The fool," said Jonathan, "he thinks the horse can swim against the current out there!"

Park had already thrown off his helmet and cloak and boots, now he sat there on his horse's back in just a shirt and pants, trying to force the horse down into the river, a pretty little black mare she was. Park shouted and kicked and urged her on, but the mare wouldn't go. She was scared. Then he beat her. He didn't have a whip. He beat her on the head with his fists, and I heard Jonathan sob, exactly like the time on the square.

At last Park got what he wanted. The mare neighed and was terrified, but she rushed into the river just because that madman wanted it. It was horrible to watch it all. And to see how she struggled, as the current took her.

"She'll drift right to us," said Jonathan. "Park can do whatever he wants — he'll never get her to the rock!"

But she tried, she really did! Oh, how she struggled, the poor mare, and how deathly frightened, when she realized that the river was stronger than her.

Even Park finally understood that now it was a matter of life or death. Then he wanted her to go back to the bank, but soon he noticed that it wouldn't work. No, because the current didn't want what he did! The current wanted to pull him to Karma Falls, and he deserved it. But the mare, I pitied her. She was completely helpless now. They came drifting toward us, exactly as Jonathan had said, soon they would pass us and disappear. I could see the terror in Park's eyes, he knew where he was headed.

I turned my head to see Jonathan, and shouted out

when I saw him. Because he was hanging from a branch, dangling over the water as far as he could go. He hung there upside down, with his legs bent around the tree branch, and just as Park went under him, Jonathan grabbed him by the hair and dragged him in, so that he could grip a branch.

And then Jonathan called to the mare:

"Come, little mare, come here!"

She had already drifted past, but she tried wildly to get to him. She didn't have that oaf Park on her back now, still she was close to sinking, but then somehow Jonathan grabbed her reins and began tugging on them. It became a tug of war between life and death, because the river didn't want to loosen its grip, it wanted both the mare and Jonathan.

I grew quite wild and I shouted to Park:

"Help them, you ox, help!"

He had crawled up into the tree, he sat there safe and sound and very close to Jonathan, but the fool did nothing to help him. He leaned forward and shouted:

"Let the horse go! There are two others up in the forest, I can take one of them instead! Just let go!"

You become strong, when you're angry, I've always heard, and you could say that Park helped in that way, so that Jonathan was able to haul in the mare.

But afterward he said to Park:

"You numbskull, do you think I saved your life so that you could steal my horse, don't you feel ashamed?"

Maybe Park was ashamed, I don't know. He said nothing, he didn't ask who we were or anything. He just climbed up the slope with his poor mare, and after that the whole troop disappeared almost at once.

We made a campfire above Karma Falls that evening. And I am sure that no fire, in any time or in any world has burned at such a campsite as where we lit ours.

It was a terrible place, horrible and beautiful like nowhere else in heaven or on earth, I think. The mountains and the river and the falls, they were too grand and enormous, all of them. Again it was like a dream, and I said to Jonathan:

"I can't believe this place is really here! It's a little bit like something out of a dream from ancient times. I'm sure of it."

We stood on the bridge, the rope bridge Tengil had had built over the chasm that divided the lands.

Karmanyaka and Nangiyala, on either side of the river of The Ancient Rivers.

The river, it came rushing deep down into the chasm under the bridge and then cast itself, roaring down Karma Falls, into an even worse and more terrible abyss.

I asked Jonathan:

"How could anyone even build a bridge over such a frightening abyss?"

"Well, I want to know that, too," he said. "And how many human lives it took, while they built it, how many fell down with a cry and disappeared into Karma Falls, that's what I want to know, too."

I shivered. I think I heard cries still echoing between the mountain walls.

We were so close to Tengil's land now. On the other side of the bridge, I could see a winding path leading up through the mountains. The Ancient Mountains in Karmanyaka.

"If you follow that path, you'll come to Tengil's castle," said Jonathan.

I shivered even more. But I thought things could go as they pleased tomorrow — tonight I would sit by the campfire with Jonathan, for the first time in my life.

We made our fire on a rock ledge high above the falls. Close to the bridge. But I sat with my back to everything. I didn't want to see the bridge to Tengil's land or anything else either. I just saw the light from the fire as it flickered along the mountain walls. It was beautiful and a little frightening, too. And I saw Jonathan's kind, handsome face in the firelight and the horses which stood resting a little farther away.

"This here is much better than my first campfire," I said. "Because now I'm sitting here with you, Jonathan!"

Wherever I was, I felt secure as long as Jonathan was with me, and I was happy to finally sit by a campfire with him, like we had talked about so much, when we lived on Earth.

"The days of campfires and the time of sagas, do you remember what you said?" I asked Jonathan.

"Yes, I remember," said Jonathan. "But I didn't know then that there would be evil sagas here in Nangiyala."

"Do you think it must it always be like this?" I asked.

He sat quietly for a while and stared into the fire, and then he said:

"No, once the final battle is over, Nangiyala will became a land where the sagas are beautiful again and life is simple and easy to live, as it was before."

The fire flared up, and in the light I saw how tired and sad he was.

"But the final battle, you see Scotty, it can only be an evil saga of death and death and death. That's why Orvar must lead the battle, not me. Because I'm not able to kill anyone."

No, I know that you couldn't, I thought. And then I asked him:

"Why did you save Park's life, was that so good?"

"I don't know if it was such a good thing to do," said Jonathan. "But there are things you *have* to do, otherwise you're not a human being, just a piece of dirt. I've said this to you before."

"But what if he'd realized who you were?" I said. "And they had caught you!"

"Well, then they would've caught Lionheart and not a piece of dirt," said Jonathan.

Our fire burned down, and darkness sank over the mountains. At first, the dusk made everything seem friendly and kind and pleasant for a time. But then came a black, roaring darkness, in which you only heard Karma Falls and couldn't see the smallest light anywhere.

I crept as close to Jonathan as I could go. We sat there leaning against the mountain wall and talked to each other in the darkness. I wasn't scared, but I felt a strange anxiety come over me. We ought to sleep, said Jonathan. But I knew that I couldn't sleep. I could hardly talk either, because of my anxiety. It was not because of the darkness, but something else, I didn't know what. And yet I had Jonathan next to me.

Then there came lightning and thunder, which boomed along the mountain walls. And then it was on top of us. A storm, I knew it wasn't like any other storm. Thunder came rolling over the mountain with a roar, so that you couldn't even hear Karma Falls any more, and flashes of fire chased each other. Sometimes there was a blazing light, and then in the next instant an even darker darkness. It was as if a night from ancient times had fallen over us.

Then came a flash of lightning, more terrible than any other. In the blink of an eye it blazed, throwing light over everything that was there.

And then, in that light, I saw Katla. *I saw Katla.*

CHAPTER THIRTEEN

Y ES, I SAW KATLA, AND THEN I DON'T KNOW WHAT happened next. I just sank into the black depths and didn't wake up until the thunderstorm passed and it was already beginning to lighten over the mountaintops. I was lying with my head on Jonathan's knee, and terror washed over me as soon as I remembered — there, far away on the other side of the river, was where Katla had stood, on a cliff high over Karma Falls. I moaned when I remembered it, and Jonathan tried to comfort me.

"She isn't there any more. She's gone now."

But I cried and asked him:

"How can something like Katla exist? Is it...a monster, or what is it?"

"Yes, she is a monster," said Jonathan. "A dragon, risen from ancient times, that's what she is and she's as cruel as Tengil himself."

"Where did he get her?" I asked.

"She came out of Katla Cavern, that's what some believe," said Jonathan. "Down there, she once fell asleep back in ancient times, she slept for thousands and thousands of years and no one knew she existed. But

168

one morning she woke up, a terrible morning, she came slithering into Tengil's castle blowing her deadly fire at everyone. They fell right and left, wherever she went."

"Why didn't she kill Tengil?" I asked.

"Tengil fled for his life through all of the castle's rooms. When she closed in, he pulled out his battle horn to call his soldiers for help, and when he blew the horn..."

"What happened then?" I asked.

"Then Katla came crawling to him like a dog. And since that day she obeys Tengil. And only Tengil. She is scared of his horn. When he blows it, she blindly obeys."

It lightened more and more. The mountaintop over in Karmanyaka glowed like Katla's fire. And Karmanyaka was where we were going. I was scared, oh, how I was scared! Who knew where Katla was lying in wait? Where was she, where did she live, did she live in Katla Cavern and how could Orvar be there? I asked Jonathan and he told me how things were.

Katla didn't live in Katla Cavern. She had never returned there after her ancient sleep, no, Tengil kept her chained in a cave near Karma Falls. In this cave, she stood bound by a chain of gold, Jonathan said, and there she stayed, except when Tengil took her with him, to strike terror in the people he wanted to terrorize.

"I saw her in Wild Rose Valley one time," said Jonathan.

"And then you screamed?" I said.

"Yes, then I screamed," he said.

Terror grew inside me.

"I'm so scared, Jonathan, Katla is coming to kill us."

Again he tried to calm me.

"But she is chained. She can't go farther than her chains reach. No farther than the cliff where you saw her. She almost always stands there and stares down into Karma Falls."

"Why does she do that?" I said.

"I don't know," said Jonathan. "Maybe she is searching for Karm."

"Who is Karm?" I asked.

"Oh, that's just Elfrida's talk," said Jonathan. "No one has ever seen Karm. He doesn't exist. But Elfrida says that he lived in Karma Falls once, in ancient times, and that Katla hated him then and could never forget it. That's why she stands there and stares."

"Who was he, how could he live in such a hellish falls?" I asked.

"He was a monster, too," said Jonathan. "A serpent, as long as the river is wide, Elfrida says. But it's just an old tale, you know."

"Maybe he's no more a story than Katla?" I said.

He didn't answer, but he said:

"Do you know what Elfrida told me? While you were walking in the forest picking strawberries. She said that when she was little, they used to frighten children with Karm and Katla. The saga of the dragon in Katla Cavern and the serpent in Karma Falls, she heard it many times as a child and enjoyed it, just because it was so horrible. It was an old story, that people have used to frighten children throughout time, Elfrida said."

"Couldn't Katla have stayed in her cavern then?" I said. "And just kept on being a story!"

"Well, that's what Elfrida thought too," said Jonathan.

I shivered, it occurred to me that Karmanyaka was a land full of monsters, and I didn't want to be there. But I had to go there now.

We fortified ourselves first, with our provisions. Though we saved something for Orvar to eat. Because in Katla Cavern there was only starvation, Jonathan said.

Grim and Fyalar drank rain water that had collected in the crevices. The pastures were poor for them to graze in, up here in the mountains. But by the bridge a little grass grew, so I think they were fairly well satisfied when we left.

And so we rode over the bridge. Toward Karmanyaka. Tengil's land and the monsters' land. I was so scared that I trembled. The serpent, I didn't seriously believe that he existed, but I still thought about him, what if he suddenly hurled himself up out of the chasm and pulled us down from the bridge to perish in Karma Falls? And Katla, I dreaded her most of all. Maybe she was waiting for us now on Tengil's shore, with her cruel fangs and her deadly fire. Oh, how I was scared!

But we went over the bridge, and I didn't see Katla. She wasn't standing on her cliff, and I said to Jonathan:

"No, she isn't there!"

And yet she was there! Not on the cliff, but her terrible head stuck out from behind a large stone next to the path up toward Tengil's castle. Then we saw her. And she saw us. And then she let out a cry that could've torn down the mountain. A spray of fire and smoke poured out of her nostrils, she snorted with rage and pulled her chain, tugging and pulling, and shrieking again.

Grim and Fyalar were terrified, we could hardly hold them. And my terror wasn't any less. I begged and asked Jonathan if we could turn back to Nangiyala. But he said:

"We can't fail Orvar! Don't be scared, Katla can't reach us even though she tugs and pulls on her chain."

Yet we must hurry, he said, because Katla's cries were a signal that would be heard up in Tengil's castle, and soon there would be a swarm of Tengil's soldiers all over us if we didn't make time to flee and hide in the mountains.

And we rode. On wretched, narrow, steep mountain trails, we rode so that sparks flew, here and there among the rocks to confuse any pursuers. Every minute I expected to hear horses galloping behind us, and shouts from Tengil's soldiers coming after us with spears and arrows and swords. But none came. It was probably hard to follow someone among the many cliffs and mountains in Karmanyaka. The hunted could easily escape here.

When had ridden for a long time, I asked Jonathan: "Where are we going?"

"To Katla Cavern, of course," he said. "We're almost there now. Katla Mountain is right in front of your nose."

Well, so it was. In front of us was a low, flat mountain with steep slopes dropping straight down. Only in our direction they didn't drop off so steeply. We could easily make our way up, if we wanted to. And we wanted to, because we had to cross over the mountain, Jonathan said.

"The entrance lies on the other side, out by the

river," he said. "And I must see what is going on there."

"Jonathan, do you really believe that we'll ever get inside of Katla Cavern?" I said.

He had told me about the huge copper door that closed off the entrance to the cave, and about Tengil's men who stood on watch outside, night and day. How, in all the world, would we get inside?

He didn't answer that. He just said that now we would hide the horses, because they couldn't climb the mountain.

We led them to a sheltered crevice right below Katla Mountain and left them there, the horses and packs and everything. Jonathan petted Grim and said:

"Wait here, we're only going out to investigate."

I didn't like the idea of investigating. Because I didn't want to be separated from Fyalar. But it couldn't be helped.

It took us a good while to reach the mountain plateau, and I was tired when we finally got there. Jonathan said that we could rest a little, and I immediately threw myself flat on the ground. Jonathan did too, and we lay there, up on Katla Mountain, with the wide sky above us and Katla Cavern right below us. Yes, it was strange I thought, somewhere beneath us inside the mountain was that horrible cavern with all its passages and caves, where so many people had wasted away and died. And here outside, butterflies fluttered around in the sunshine, the sky above us was blue with little white clouds, and around us were flowers and grass. It was strange, flowers and grass grew on the roof of Katla Cavern!

It came to me, that since so many people had died in Katla Cavern, then Orvar might also be dead, and I asked Jonathan what he believed. But he didn't answer. He just lay there and stared up into the sky, he was thinking about something, I realized. At last he said:

"If it's true that Katla slept her ancient sleep in Katla Cavern, how did she get out, when she woke up? The copper door was already there then. Tengil has always used Katla Cavern as a prison."

"While Katla laid asleep, inside there?" I said.

"Yes, while Katla laid asleep inside there," said Jonathan. "But no one knew it."

I shivered. I couldn't imagine anything worse. Think of sitting imprisoned in Katla Cavern, and seeing a dragon creep right by!

But Jonathan had other thoughts in his head.

"She must've come out another way," he said. "And I *must* find that way, even if I have to look for a year."

We couldn't rest long, Jonathan was uneasy. We were approaching Katla Cavern. It was just a short walk over the mountain. We already saw the river far down below us and Nangiyala on the other side, oh, how I longed to be there!

"Look, Jonathan," I said, "I see the willow tree where we swam! There, on the other side of the river!"

It was like receiving a greeting from across the water, a small green greeting from the riverbank.

But Jonathan signaled to me to be quiet. He was afraid that someone would hear us. We were so close now. Katla Mountain ended here with a vertical drop, and in the mountain wall below us was the copper door to Katla Cavern, Jonathan said, although we couldn't see it from up here.

But we could see the soldiers on guard. Three of Tengil's men, I only had to see their black helmets for my heart to begin thumping.

We crept on our stomachs toward the slope so that we could peer down at them. And if they had peered up, they would've seen us. But there couldn't be more worthless guards. They did not look here or there. They just sat and played dice and didn't care about anything else. No enemy had ever penetrated through the copper door, so why should they keep watch?

Just then we saw the door swing open down there, and someone came out of the cavern — one of Tengil's men! He carried an empty food bowl, but he tossed it away from himself onto the ground. The door closed again behind him, and we heard it lock.

"Well, now the swine's been fed for the last time," he said.

The others laughed at that, and one of them said:

"Does he know this is a special day — his last to live! Did you tell him that Katla is waiting for him tonight, when darkness falls?"

"Yes, and do you know what he said then? 'Yes, at last,' he said. And then he asked to send word to Wild Rose Valley, how did it go again? 'Orvar may die, but freedom never!' "

"Kiss me," said the other, "that's what he can say to Katla tonight, and he'll get to hear her answer."

I looked at Jonathan. He had become pale.

"Come," he said. "We must leave here."

And we crept away from the slope as quietly and quickly as we could, and when we knew that we were out of sight, we ran. We ran the whole way back and didn't stop until we were with Grim and Fyalar again.

We sat in the crevice with the horses, because now we didn't know what we could do. Jonathan was so sad, and I couldn't do anything to comfort him, I could only be sad too. I knew how much he mourned for Orvar. He had believed that he could help him, and now he didn't think so anymore.

"Orvar, my friend, whom I never got to meet," he said. "Tonight you'll die, and what will happen to Nangiyala's green valleys then?"

We ate a little bread which we shared with Grim and Fyalar. I wanted to have a few sips of goat milk too, we had saved some.

"Not yet, Scotty," said Jonathan. "Tonight when darkness has fallen, then I'll give you every drop. But not before."

He sat there for a long time, so quiet and in poor spirits, but at last he said:

"It's like searching for a needle in a haystack, I know. But we must still try."

"Try what?" I asked.

"To locate where Katla came out," he said.

Though he didn't believe in it himself, I noticed.

"If we had a year," he said. "Then maybe! But we only have a day."

Just as he had said that, something happened. In the narrow crevice, where we sat, some thick bushes grew along the far end of the mountain wall, and out of those bushes a terrified fox suddenly appeared. It slunk past us and was gone almost before we had seen it.

"Where in the world did that fox come from?" said Jonathan. "I have to find out."

He disappeared behind the bushes. I stayed put and waited. But he took such a long time and it was so quiet, that finally I became worried.

"Where are you, Jonathan?" I shouted.

Then I definitely got an answer. He sounded very excited.

"Do you know where that fox came from? From inside the mountain! Do you understand, Scotty, from inside Katla Mountain! There is a large cavern in there!"

Maybe everything was already predetermined in the sagas from ancient times. Maybe it had already been predetermined that Jonathan would rescue Orvar for the sake of Wild Rose Valley. And maybe a secret being from the saga guided our steps, but we didn't realize it. How else could Jonathan have found a way into Katla Cavern right where we had put our horses? It was just as strange as when I ended up at Mattias's farm, among all the houses in Wild Rose Valley, and no other place.

Katla's passage out of Kata Cavern, this must be what Jonathan had found, we didn't think it could be anything else. It was a hole right through the mountain wall. Not large at all. But big enough for a starving dragon to pass through, Jonathan said, if she woke after thousands of years and found her usual path closed off by the copper door.

And big enough for us! I stared into the dark hole. How many sleeping dragons were in there, do you think? Dragons who would wake up if you entered and happened to step on them. That's what I wondered.

Then I felt Jonathan's arm around my shoulders.

"Scotty," he said, "I don't know what waits there inside, in the darkness, but I'm going in there now."

"I will, too," I said, though I knew my voice quavered a little.

Jonathan touched my cheek with his finger, as he did sometimes.

"Are you sure you wouldn't rather wait here with the horses?"

"Haven't I said that wherever you go, I'll follow?" I said.

"Yes, you've said that," said Jonathan, and he sounded quite happy.

"Because I want to be with you," I said, "even if it's a chasm in a land underground."

Katla Cavern was such a chasm. Creeping through that black hole, it was like creeping through an evil, black dream you couldn't wake up from, it was like going from sunlight to perpetual night.

All of Katla Cavern was nothing but an old, dead dragon's lair, I thought, still smoldering with evil from ancient times. Thousands of dragon eggs had probably hatched here and cruel dragons crawled out like an army platoon to begin killing everyone that got in their way.

An old dragon's lair, Tengil would think it was suitable for a prison. I shivered, when I thought of everything he had done to people inside here. I felt the air was thick with old, dried evil. And I heard strange whisperings in the midst of the horrible silence surrounding us. Far inside the cavern's depths, it whispered, and I felt that it was all the pain and all the tears and all the death that Katla Cavern had experienced under Tengil's rule. I wanted to ask Jonathan if he also heard the whispering, but I let it be. Because it was probably just my imagination.

"Now, Scotty, we're going on a walk that you'll probably never forget," said Jonathan.

And so it was. We had to cross through the entire mountain to reach the cave prison, just inside the copper door, where Orvar was. This was the cave folks meant, when they spoke about Katla Cavern, Jonathan said, because they they didn't know of any other cave. And we didn't know either if it was really possible to reach underground. But the way was long, we knew. We had wandered this stretch up the mountain before. It would be seven times worse fumbling down here in the dark winding passages, without any light other than the torches we carried with us.

Oh, it was horrible to watch the torchlight flickering along the cavern walls. It could only light up a little, little bit of the great darkness around us, and that's why everything outside the light felt even more dangerous. Who knows, I thought, maybe it was full of dragons and serpents and monsters lying in wait for us in their dark cave. I was also so scared that we would get lost in the winding passages, but Jonathan made black soot marks on the cavern walls with his torch as we went, so that we could find our way back.

Walk, Jonathan said, but we didn't do much walking. We crept and crawled and climbed and swam and

jumped and scaled and struggled and slaved and more, that's what we did. What a walk! And what caves! Sometimes we came to caverns so large that we couldn't see the other end of them, we realized how huge the rooms were only from the echo. Sometimes we went where you couldn't stand up, but had to crawl on your stomach like any other dragon. Sometimes the way was blocked by an underground stream, which we had to swim to get across. And worse than anything else — sometimes gaping chasms opened in front of our feet. I almost fell down into one of these chasms. I was carrying the torch then, and I tripped. Jonathan grabbed me just as I would've gone down into the abyss. And that's when I happened to drop the torch. We saw it fall, like a stream of fire, deeper and deeper and deeper, and at last it disappeared. And so we were in the darkness. It was utterly the worst darkness in all the world. I dared not move or talk or think, I tried to forget that I existed and that I stood there in the blackest darkness of all, next to a chasm. But I heard Jonathan's voice next to me. He finally lit the other torch we had with us. And meanwhile he talked to me, talked and talked, quite calmly. That was why I didn't die from terror, I believe.

And so we slaved on. How long, I don't know. In the depths of Katla Cavern you didn't know anything about time. It felt as if we had wandered in there for an eternity, and I began to be scared that we wouldn't get there until it was too late. Maybe it was already nighttime, maybe darkness had already fallen out there. And Orvar...maybe he was already with Katla now!

I asked Jonathan if he thought so.

"I don't know," he said. "But if you don't want to go crazy, don't think about it now."

We came to a narrow, winding passage that never wanted to end and that just became narrower and tighter bit by bit. It shrunk both in height and width, until you could hardly squeeze through any longer, and in the end it became just a hole, you had to crawl to get through it.

But on the other side of the hole, suddenly we were in a large cavern. We didn't know how large it was, because the light from the torch didn't reach far. But Jonathan tried out an echo.

"Hohoho," he shouted, and we heard the echo answer, "Hohoho" many times and from many directions.

But then we heard something more. Another voice far away in the darkness.

"Hohoho," it copied. "What do you want, you who enter here in such a strange way, with a torch and light?"

"I'm searching for Orvar," said Jonathan.

"Orvar is here," said the voice. "And who are you?"

"I'm Jonathan Lionheart," said Jonathan. "And with me is my brother, Karl Lionheart. We've come to rescue you, Orvar."

"Too late," said the voice, "too late — but thanks in any case!"

He had hardly said that before we heard the copper door open with a crash. Jonathan threw down the torch and trampled it to put it out. Then we stood still and waited.

And in through the door came one of Tengil's men with a lantern in his hand. I began to cry quietly to myself, not because I was scared, but for Orvar's sake. How could we have such rotten luck, that they would come to take him right now!

"Orvar of Wild Rose Valley, get ready," said Tengil's man. "You'll meet Katla before long. The black escorts are on the way."

In the light from his lantern, we saw a large wooden cage with thick timbers, and we realized that Orvar was held prisoner there like an animal.

Tengil's man put the lantern down on the ground next to the cage.

"You may have a lantern during your last hour. Tengil has decided this, in all his grace. So that you'll become accustomed to the light again and can see Katla when you meet her. That's what you want, right?"

He bellowed with laughter and then he disappeared out through the doorway. Behind him, it closed again with a crash.

By then we were already in front of the cage with Orvar, and we saw him in the light of the lantern. It was pitiful. He could hardly move, but he still crept up to the bars and stretched out his hands to us through the timbers.

"Jonathan Lionheart," he said. "I heard much about you, back home in Wild Rose Valley. And now you've come here!"

"Yes, now I've come here," said Jonathan, and then I heard him crying a little, too, because of Orvar's misery. But then he pulled out a knife from his belt and went to work on the cage.

"Slash it, Scotty! Help!" he said. And I slashed with

my knife too. Although what could we do with a pair of knives? We needed an axe and saw.

But we cut with the knives until our hands became bloody. We cut and cried, we knew that we had arrived too late. Orvar knew it too, but maybe he wanted to think differently, that it wasn't true, because he was grunting with excitement inside his cage, and sometimes he mumbled:

"Hurry! Hurry!"

And we did, so that the blood ran. We cut wildly and every moment we waited for the door to open and for the black escorts to come in and then it would be the end for Orvar and for us and for all of Wild Rose Valley.

They won't have only one to take away, I thought. Katla will get three tonight!

I felt that I couldn't stand it any longer, my hands trembled so much that I could hardly hold the knife. And Jonathan shouted with rage, he was furious that the timbers wouldn't give, however much we slashed at them. He kicked at them, screamed and kicked and slashed again and kicked again, and then finally there was a crash. Yes, finally one of the timbers snapped. And then one more. It was enough.

"Now, Orvar, now," said Jonathan. But he only got a gasp in reply. Then he crept inside the cage and dragged Orvar out, he couldn't stand or walk on his legs. I could hardly either, at this point, but I staggered in front shining the lantern, and Jonathan began dragging Orvar away toward our tunnel to safety. He was tired now and he panted too, well, all three of us panted like hunted animals, and that's how we felt too, at least I did.

184

However he managed it, Jonathan succeeded in dragging Orvar across the entire cavern and he succeeded in forcing himself through the hole and amazingly he was able to take Orvar with him, who was more dead than alive. I was almost, too — and now it was my turn to crawl through the hole. But I never had time to get that far. Because we heard the door creaking, and then it was as if I ran out of energy. I couldn't move at all.

"Quick, quick, the lantern," panted Jonathan, and I held it out to him, although my hands shook. The lantern needed to be hidden, the smallest stream of light would be enough to give us away.

The black escorts — they were already inside the cavern now. And Tengil's men, too, with lanterns in their hands. They were so fearfully bright. But over in our corner it was dark. And Jonathan began to pull me out by the arms and dragged me through the hole, into the dark passage behind. And there we lay, all three panting and we heard the cries:

"He's escaped! He's escaped!"

CHAPTER FOURTEEN

*T*HAT NIGHT WE CARRIED ORVAR THROUGH THE
underground. Jonathan did. He dragged Orvar
through hell, it couldn't be called anything else. I was
just able to drag myself, and hardly that.

"He's escaped! He's escaped!" they cried, and when it
became quiet we waited for pursuers. But they didn't
come. Still, even Tengil's men must've figured out that
there was a hole to crawl through out of Katla Cavern,
when we disappeared. And the hole couldn't be that
hard to find. But they were cowards, Tengil's men, they
dared to attack an enemy as a pack, but none of them
dared to crawl first into the narrow passage, where an
unknown enemy waited. No, it was because every single
one of them was a coward, why else would they allow us
to escape so easily? No one had ever run away from
Katla Cavern before, and how would they explain
Orvar's escape to Tengil? That's what I wondered. But
that was their problem, Jonathan said, we had more
than enough of our own.

186

Not until we had dragged ourselves through the long, narrow passage did we dare to stop and catch our breath for a while. It was necessary for Orvar's sake. Jonathan gave him goat milk that was sour and bread that was soggy, still Orvar said:

"I've never had a better meal!"

Jonathan rubbed Orvar's legs for a while, to bring life back to them and he recovered a little. Although he couldn't walk, just crawl.

He learned from Jonathan which way we needed to travel, and Jonathan asked him, if he still wanted to go farther that night.

"Yes, yes, yes," said Orvar. "I will crawl on my knees home to Wild Rose Valley, if I have to. I won't lie here calmly waiting for Tengil's bloodhounds to come snarling after us in this passageway."

It was already noticeable who he was. Not a subdued prisoner, but a rebel and freedom fighter. Orvar of Wild Rose Valley, when I saw his eyes in the lantern's light, then I understood how Tengil could be scared of him. Even though he was still weak, he had some sort of fire burning inside, and it was probably thanks to this fire that he lived through our hellish night. Because this had to have been the worst night in the world.

It was as long as an eternity and full of terror. But when you become sufficiently tired, you don't have the energy to care about anything. Not even if bloodhounds are coming. Yes, I certainly heard the hounds coming, growling and barking, but I didn't have the *energy* to be scared. Besides, soon it became quiet. Not one bloodhound dared go far into the chasm, where we were crawling around.

Far, far we crawled and when we finally crawled out into the daylight by Grim and Fyalar, broken and scraped and bloody and soaked to the skin and as good as dead from exhaustion, night was over and morning already here. Orvar stretched out his arms, he wanted to hug the ground and the sky and everything he saw, but his arms fell down, he was already asleep. We sank into a deep slumber, all three, and knew nothing until it was almost evening. Then I woke. Fyalar pushed me with his nose. Surely he thought that I had slept long enough.

Jonathan was also awake.

"We must be out of Karmanyaka, before it gets dark," he said. "Or we won't find the way."

He woke Orvar. And then Orvar came to life and sat up and looked around and remembered and understood that he was no longer in Katla Cavern, tears came into his eyes.

"Free," he mumbled, "free!"

And he took Jonathan's hands and held them for a long time in his.

"You've given me back my life and my freedom," he said and he thanked me too, though I hadn't done much but be in the way.

Surely Orvar felt as I did, when I was freed from my sickness and came to Cherry Valley, and I wished so much, that he would also reach *his* valley, alive and free. But we weren't there yet. We were still in Karmanyaka's mountains, now probably teeming with Tengil's soldiers, who were searching for him. It was only luck that they hadn't found us in our crevice, while we slept.

We sat there in our crevice and ate the last of our bread. And then and there Orvar said:

"I'm alive! I am free and I live!"

Because he had been the last prisoner still left alive in Katla Cavern. All the others, one after one, had been offered to Katla.

"But you can rely on Tengil," he said. "Believe me, he'll see to it that Katla Cavern won't stand empty for long."

Again the tears came to his eyes.

"Oh, my Wild Rose Valley," he said, "how long will you grieve under Tengil?"

He wanted to hear about everything that had happened in Nangiyala's valleys during his imprisonment. About Sofia and about Mattias and about everything that Jonathan had done. And Jonathan told him. Also about Jossi. I almost thought Orvar would die in front of our eyes. When he found out that it was because of Jossi that he had suffered for so long in Katla Cavern. It was a long time before he was himself and could talk again, and then he said:

"My life means nothing. But what Jossi has done to Wild Rose Valley, for that he can never make amends or be forgiven."

"Forgiven or not, he's probably gotten his punishment by now," said Jonathan. "You'll never see Jossi again!"

But a fury had come over Orvar. He wanted to leave, it was as if he wanted to begin the freedom fight already, this evening, and he swore at his legs which carried him so poorly. Though he tried and tried, and at last succeeded in raising himself up and he stood on them. He was proud when he could show us that. And he certainly was a sight as he stood there and swayed back and forth as if he would blow down. You had to smile, when you saw him.

"Orvar," said Jonathan, "anyone can tell from far away that you're a prisoner from Katla Cavern."

And it was true. We were bloody and dirty, all three, but Orvar was the worst. His clothes were in rags, and his face was hardly visible, because of his beard and all his hair. You could only see his eyes. His intense, burning eyes.

A stream ran through our crevice, and there we washed away all the dirt and blood. Time after time, I dipped my face in the water. It was wonderful. It felt like I was washing away all of Katla Cavern.

Then Orvar borrowed my knife and cut off much of his beard and hair, so that he looked a little less like an escaped prisoner. And from his pack, Jonathan took the Tengil helmet and cloak that had gotten him out of Wild Rose Valley.

"Here, Orvar, put these on," he said. "Then maybe they'll believe that you're one of Tengil's men who has taken two prisoners and are on your way with them somewhere."

And Orvar pulled on the helmet and cloak, but he didn't like it.

"This is the first and last time you'll see me in these clothes," he said. "They smell of oppression and cruelty."

"They can smell how they like," said Jonathan, "if they can help you get home to Wild Rose Valley."

It was time for us to leave now. In a few hours the sun would go down, and when it became dark in the mountains, no one could make their way on these dangerous paths.

Jonathan looked serious. He knew what awaited us, and I heard what he said to Orvar:

"I believe the next two hours will determine Wild Rose Valley's fate. Can you manage that long on horseback?"

"Yes, yes, yes," said Orvar. "For ten hours if you like."

He would ride Fyalar. Jonathan helped him up on the horse's back. Then he was an entirely different Orvar, almost as if he grew in the saddle and became strong, yes, Orvar was brave and strong just like Jonathan. I was the only one who wasn't brave at all. But when we had mounted and I was sitting there with my arms around Jonathan's waist and my forehead leaning against his back, it was as if a little of his strength flowed over me, and I wasn't so scared any more. Still, I couldn't help thinking how nice it would be if we didn't always need to be strong and brave. If only we could be together again like the first days in Cherry Valley, oh, it seemed so long ago now!

Then we began our journey. We rode toward the sunset, toward the bridge. In Karmanyaka's mountains there were many paths and they all looked the same. No one except Jonathan could've found the right way in this mess. But he found it in some strange way, which was lucky for us.

I searched for Tengil's men until my eyes stung. But none appeared. Only Orvar rode behind us wearing his horrible helmet and black cloak. My terror heightened every time I happened to turn my head and saw him, I had learned to be fearful of that helmet and everyone who wore them.

We rode and rode, and nothing happened. It was so calm and serene and beautiful everywhere we went. A quiet evening in the mountains, you could call it, I thought. If only it weren't so wrong. How easily something could turn up in the quiet and stillness, and all we felt was an awful tension. Even Jonathan was worried and on watch every moment.

"If only we make it across the bridge," said Jonathan, "then the worst will be over."

"How soon will we be there?" I asked.

"Within a half an hour, if all goes well," said Jonathan.

But then we saw them. A troop of Tengil's men, six men with spears on black horses. They emerged where the trail curved around the mountain wall, and they came trotting right toward us.

"Now, it's a matter of life or death," said Jonathan. "Over here, Orvar!"

Orvar hastily rode up from behind us, and Jonathan threw the reins over to him so that we would look a little more like prisoners.

They still hadn't noticed us. But it was too late to escape. And there was nowhere to escape. The only thing we could do was to ride on and hope that Orvar's cloak and helmet would fool them.

"I'll never be taken alive," said Orvar. "I want you to know that, Lionheart!"

As calmly as we could, we rode toward our enemies. Closer and closer we went. My back tingled, and I had time to think that if we were caught now, we could've

just as easily stayed in Katla Cavern and avoided being
tormented during the long night to no avail.

Then we met. They slowed down their horses to pass
us on the narrow path. The one who rode in front was
an old friend. It was none other than Park.

But Park didn't look at us. He only looked at Orvar.
And, just as they rode past each other, he asked:

"Have you heard if they've found him yet?"

"No, I haven't heard anything," said Orvar.

"Where are you going?" asked Park.

"I have a few prisoners," said Orvar, and he didn't
tell Park anything more. The we rode on, just as quick
as we dared.

194

"Turn around carefully, Scotty, and see what they're doing," said Jonathan. And I did as he said.

"They're riding away," I said.

"Thank goodness," said Jonathan.

But he rejoiced too soon. Because now I saw that they had stopped, and were all looking back at us.

"They've started thinking," said Jonathan.

And evidently they had.

"Stop for a minute," shouted Park. "Listen, I want to take a closer look at you and your prisoners!"

Orvar clenched his teeth.

"Ride on, Jonathan," he said. "Or we're dead!"

And we rode.

Then Park and the whole trooped turned, yes, they turned around and set out after us, the manes of their horses flowing.

"Now, Grim, show them what you can do," said Jonathan.

And you too, my Fyalar, I thought and just wished that I had gotten to ride him.

There were no better sprinters than Grim and Fyalar, oh, how they flew along the path, they knew it was now a matter of life and death! Our pursuers were after us. We heard thundering hooves sometimes closer, sometimes farther away, but persevering, never becoming silent. Because now Park knew whom he was hunting, and none of Tengil's men could let such a quarry slip away, that would be quite something to haul back to Tengil in his castle.

We had them at our heels, as we galloped over the bridge, and a pair of spears were thrown at us. But they didn't reach us.

Now we were over on the Nangiyala side, and the worst should be over, Jonathan had said. But on the contrary, I didn't notice it. The witch hunt continued farther along the river. High up on to the bank, the riding trail turned leading toward Wild Rose Valley, and we sprinted there. We had traveled by here on another summer night, it easily seemed like a thousand years ago now, when we had come riding along at dusk, Jonathan and I, slowly riding on the way to our first campfire. That's how you should travel by the river, not like now so that the horses were almost dropping.

Orvar rode the wildest. Because now he was riding home to Wild Rose Valley. Jonathan couldn't stay with him. And Park was gaining on us too, I couldn't understand why. Until it finally dawned on me, it was my fault. There wasn't a swifter rider than Jonathan, no one could reach him, if he were alone on a horse. But now he had to think of me all the time, and it hindered him.

This ride would determine the fate of Wild Rose Valley, Jonathan had said. And I would determine how it would end, which was horrible! More and more, I felt that it would end badly. Every time I turned around and looked back, the black helmets had come a little closer to us. Sometimes they were obscured behind a hill or trees, but then relentlessly they were there again, nearer and nearer.

Jonathan knew as well as I did now, that we couldn't save ourselves. Not both of us. And it was necessary for Jonathan to escape. I couldn't let him be captured for my sake. That's why I said:

"Jonathan, do what I say, now! Let me down behind the bend, when they won't see it! And catch up to Orvar!"

He was astonished at first, I noticed. But not as amazed as I was myself.

"Do you really want to risk it?" asked Jonathan.

"No, but I still will," I said.

"Brave little Scotty," he said. "I'll come back and get you. As soon as I have Orvar safely at home with Mattias, I'll come."

"You promise," I said.

"Yes, what do you think?" he said.

Then we had reached the willow tree, where we went swimming, and I said:

"I'll hide in our tree. Return for me there!"

I didn't have time to say more, because now we were sheltered behind a hill and Jonathan reined in his horse so that I could slide off. Then he sped off again. And I quickly rolled aside down into a hollow. I lay there and heard our pursuers thunder past. I caught a quick glimpse of Park's stupid face. He was gnashing his teeth, as if he were ready to bite — and Jonathan had saved his life!

But now Jonathan had already caught up with Orvar, I saw them disappear together and I was very satisfied. Ride, little Park, I thought, if you think it'll help! Orvar and Jonathan will never see you again.

I stayed in the hollow until Park and his men were also out of sight. Then I scurried down to the river and to my tree. It was pleasant to crawl up into its green top and sit in the fork of a branch. Because I was tired now.

A little rowboat lay there and bumped against the bank by the tree. It must've pulled loosed from somewhere farther upstream. Because it wasn't moored. Whoever had lost it was probably sad now, I thought. Well, I sat there and thought a little bit about everything and looked around me. I saw the rushing water and Park's rock, the coward should be sitting out there, I thought. And so I looked at Katla Mountain on the other side of the river and wondered how anyone could imprison another person in her horrible cavern. I thought about Orvar and Jonathan too, and hoped so badly that they would escape to our underground passage, before Park caught them. And I wondered what Mattias would say, when he found Orvar inside the hideout, how happy he would be then. All of that is what I thought about.

But it began to get dark, and now it occurred to me for the first time, that I might be there the whole night.

Jonathan wouldn't come back, before it got dark. It was a little eerie, anxiety came crawling over me at the same time dusk was falling, and I felt lonely.

Then suddenly I saw a woman on horseback up on the riverbank. And it was none other than Sofia. Indeed, it was Sofia, I've never been so happy to see her than just then.

"Sofia," I cried, "Sofia, here I am!"

And I crept out of the tree and waved my arms. But it took some time before I could make her understand that it was really me.

"Oh, Karl!" she shouted, "how did you get here? And where is Jonathan? Wait, we're coming down to you, we still need to water our horses."

And then I saw two men behind her, also on horseback. I recognized the first one, it was Hubert. The other was hidden, but then he rode forward a little. And I saw him. It was Jossi.

But it *couldn't* be Jossi — I thought that I might have gone crazy and was seeing things, Sofia couldn't have come here with Jossi! What had gone wrong? Was Sofia crazy too, or had I just dreamed that Jossi was a traitor? No, no, I hadn't dreamed it, he was a traitor! And I wasn't looking at a vision, here he came, and what would happen now? Help, what would happen now?

He came riding down to the river in the twilight, and he shouted from far away:

"Well, to see little Kalle Lionheart, we meet again!"

They came, all three. I stood still down by the water and waited for them with just one thought in my head: Help, what will happen now?

They jumped off their horses, and Sofia came running over and took me in her arms. She was happy, her eyes were shining.

"Are you out hunting wolves again?" said Hubert, and he laughed.

But I stood there silently and just stared.

"Where are you going?" I managed to get out at last.

"Jossi's going to show us where we can best break through the wall," said Sofia. "When the day of our battle arrives, we must know this."

"Yes, we must," said Jossi. "We must have a clear plan before we attack."

I was raging inside. At least you have a clear plan, I thought. I knew why he was there now. He wanted to lure Sofia and Hubert into a trap. He would drag them straight into destruction, if no one stopped him. But someone *must* stop him, I thought. And then I understood: Help, I must be the one to do it! And it couldn't wait. It must be done right now. I still didn't like this idea, but I had to do it now. But how would I begin?

"Sofia, how is Bianca feeling?" I asked at last.

Then Sofia looked sad.

"Bianca never came back from Wild Rose Valley," she said. "But do you know anything about Jonathan?"

She didn't want to talk about Bianca. But I found out what I wanted to know. Bianca was dead. That was why Sofia could come here with Jossi. She had never gotten our message.

Jossi also wanted to hear, if I knew anything about Jonathan.

"He must never have been caught," he said.

"No, he wasn't," I said and looked at Jossi straight in the eyes. "He's just rescued Orvar from Katla Cavern."

Then Jossi's rosy face became pale and silent. But Sofia and Hubert cheered, oh, how they cheered! Sofia hugged me again, and Hubert said:

"That's the best news you could've given us."

They wanted to know how it had all happened. But not Jossi, he was in a hurry now.

"We can hear about it later," he said. "We must get to where we're going, before darkness falls."

Yes, because Tengil's soldiers must already lie waiting, I thought.

"Come, Karl," said Sofia, "we'll ride together on my horse, you and I."

"No," I said, "you shouldn't ride anywhere with that traitor!"

I pointed to Jossi. And I thought he would kill me. He grabbed me by the neck with his big hands and hissed:

"What are you saying! One more word and I'll smack you."

Sofia got him to release me. But she wasn't happy with me.

"Karl, it's awful to call someone a traitor, when it isn't true. But you're too little to understand what you've just said."

And Hubert, he laughed a little.

"I thought I was the traitor? I know too much and like white horses, what was it that you wrote on the kitchen wall back at home?"

"Yes, Karl, you're throwing out accusations in every

direction," said Sofia sternly. "You need to stop!"

"I ask for your forgiveness, Hubert," I said.

"Well, what about Jossi?" said Sofia.

"I won't ask for forgiveness for calling a traitor a traitor," I said.

But I couldn't get them to believe me. It was terrible, when I realized it. They wanted to follow Jossi. They were bringing about their own misfortune, but I still tried to stand up to them.

"He's luring you into a trap," I shouted. "I know it! I know it! Ask him about Veder and Kader, whom he used to meet up on the mountain! And ask him what he did, when he betrayed Orvar!"

Jossi wanted to rush at me again, but he restrained himself.

"Can we get going," he said, "or should we risk everything just because of this boy's lies?"

He gave me a look full of hatred.

"And I liked you at one time," he said.

"At one time I liked you, too," I said.

I could see how scared he was, underneath his fury. He was really in a hurry now, he needed to have Sofia captured and imprisoned, before she learned the truth. Or else it could be a matter of life and death to him.

What a relief it must've been to him that Sofia didn't want to know the truth. She relied on Jossi, as she had always done. And at first I had accused one and then another, why should she believe me?

"Come now, Karl," she said, "I will straighten this out with you later."

"There will be no 'later' if you follow Jossi," I said.

And then I cried. Nangiyala couldn't afford to lose Sofia, and here I stood and I couldn't save her. Because she didn't want to be saved.

"Come now, Karl," she said again, persistently.

But just then I remembered something.

"Jossi," I said, "open you shirt and show them what you have on your chest!"

Jossi's face went white, even Sofia and Hubert must've noticed it, and he laid his hand over his chest as if he wanted to hide something.

It was quiet for a moment. But then Hubert said with a gruff voice:

"Jossi, do as the boy says!"

Sofia stood in silence and looked at Jossi for a long time. But he turned his eyes away.

"We have to hurry," he said, and he wanted to go to his horse.

Sofia's eyes hardened.

"Not *so* fast," she said. "I'm your leader, Jossi, show me your chest!"

It was terrible to watch Jossi then. He stood there and gasped, unable to move and frightened, and he didn't know if he should run or stay. Sofia went up to him, but he knocked her out of the way with his elbow. He shouldn't have done that. She grasped him firmly and tore open his shirt.

And there on his chest was Katla's mark. A dragon's head, and it glistened like blood.

Then Sofia became even more pale than Jossi.

"Traitor," she said. "You shall be cursed for what you've done to Nangiyala's valleys!"

At last Jossi came to life. He swore and rushed toward his horse. But Hubert was already there and barred his way. Then he turned and searched wildly for another way to escape. And he saw the rowboat. With a single leap he was down in it, and before Sofia and Hubert could even make it to the bank, the current carried him beyond reach.

Then he laughed, and a horrible laugh it was.

"I'll punish you, Sofia," he shouted. "When I'm chief of Cherry Valley, I'll punish you severely."

You miserable fool, you're never coming back to Cherry Valley, I thought. You're going to Karma Falls, and nowhere else.

He tried to row, but the furious, whirling waves slashed at the boat and threw it amongst themselves, to crush it. They tore the oars from him. And then a raging wave came, knocking him down into the water. Then I cried and wanted to save him, even though he was a traitor. But I knew there was no way to rescue Jossi. It was so terrible and so sad to stand there in the darkness, watching and knowing that Jossi was completely alone and helpless out there among the swirling waves. We saw him come up once, on top of a wave. Then he sank again. And we saw him no more.

It was almost dark now, as the river of Ancient Rivers took Jossi and carried him toward Karma Falls.

CHAPTER FIFTEEN

*T*HE DAY OF BATTLE CAME AT LAST, WHICH EVERYONE had been waiting for. It was stormy over Wild Rose Valley that day, so that trees bent and broke. But it probably wasn't the type of storm Orvar meant, when he said:

"The storm of freedom shall come, and it will break our oppressors as the trees break and fall. It will go thundering forward and sweep away our slavery and make us free again at last!"

He said this in Mattias's kitchen. People came in secret to hear him and see him, yes, they wanted to see him and Jonathan.

"You two are our solace and our hope, you're all that we have," they said. And they would sneak to Mattias's farm at night, although they knew how risky it was.

"Because they want to hear about the storm of freedom just like children want to hear sagas," said Mattias.

The day of the battle was all that they thought about and longed for now. And it wasn't so strange. After Orvar's escape, Tengil was more cruel than ever. Every day he found new ways to torment and punish Wild Rose Valley, that's why they hated him more passionately now than ever, and they forged more and more weapons in the valley.

And more and more freedom fighters came from Cherry Valley to help. Sofia and Hubert had an army camp in the forest, hidden deep away with Elfrida. Some nights Sofia came through the underground passage, and in Mattias's kitchen they worked on the battle plans, she and Orvar and Jonathan.

I lay there and listened to them, because I slept on the kitchen sofa now, since Orvar needed room in the hideout. And every time Sofia came, she said:

"There's my savior! Surely I haven't forgotten to thank you, Karl?"

And then Orvar said every time, that I was the hero of Wild Rose Valley, but I thought about Jossi in the dark waters and only felt sad.

Sofia also controlled the bread in Wild Rose Valley. It came over the mountain in a cart from Cherry Valley and was smuggled through the underground passage. Mattias went around with a pack on his back and rationed it out secretly to the farms. I never knew before that people could be so happy over just a little bread. Now I saw it, because I went with Mattias on his walks. And I saw how the folks in the valley lived and listened to them talk about the battle day which they longed for so much.

206

I myself dreaded the day, but yet I almost began to long for it too. Because it was unbearable to just stay there and wait. And dangerous too, Jonathan said.

"You can't keep so much a secret for long," he said to Orvar. "Our dream of freedom can be easily crushed."

He certainly had that right. If just one of Tengil's men found the underground passage or if they renewed their search of homes again, then Jonathan and Orvar could be discovered inside the hideout. I shivered just thinking about it.

But Tengil's men must've been both blind and deaf, or else they would've noticed *something*. If they had listened a little, they would've heard how the storm of freedom began to thunder, soon to resound throughout all of Wild Rose Valley. But they didn't notice.

The evening before the day of the battle, I was lying on my sofa and couldn't sleep. Because of the storm outside and from anxiety. They decided it would begin, as dawn was breaking the next morning. Orvar and Jonathan and Mattias sat by the table and discussed it, and I was lying there and listened. It was mostly Orvar that I heard. He talked and talked, his eyes blazing. He longed for morning more than anyone else.

This is what would happen, from what I understood of their talk. The guards at the main gate and the river gate would be struck down first, so that they could be opened for Sofia and Hubert. They would ride in with their forces, Sofia through the main gate and Hubert through the river gate.

"And then we shall be victorious together or die," said Orvar.

It must happen swiftly, he said. The valley must be rid of all of Tengil's men and the gates shut again, before Tengil had time to arrive with Katla. Because there were no weapons to use against Katla. She couldn't be beaten other than through starvation, said Orvar.

"Neither spears nor arrows nor swords can hurt her," he said. "And only a single little blaze of her fire is enough to paralyze or kill anyone."

"But if Tengil has Katla over there in his mountains, what use is there to freeing Wild Rose Valley?" I asked. "With her, he can suppress you once more, like the first time."

"He has given us a wall to protect ourselves, don't forget," said Orvar. "And gates to shut against monsters! He's been kind!"

And besides, I didn't need to be worried about Tengil any more, said Orvar. That night he and Jonathan and Sofia and many others would force their way into his castle, overpowering his bodyguards and finishing him off there, before he even knew anything was wrong in the valley. And then Katla would stay bound in her cave, until she became so weak and hungry that they could kill her.

"There's no other way to get rid of this monster," said Orvar.

He talked again of how quickly they must free the valley of all of Tengil's men, and then Jonathan said:

"Free? You mean kill?"

"Yes, what else could I mean?" said Orvar.

"But I can't kill anyone," said Jonathan, "you know that Orvar!"

"Not even if it means your life?" asked Orvar.

"No, not even then," said Jonathan.

Orvar couldn't understand this and Mattias hardly could, either.

"If everyone were like you," said Orvar, "then evil would rule for all eternity!"

But then I said that if everyone were like Jonathan, then there would be no evil.

Then I didn't say anything else for the evening. Except when Mattias came and stopped by me. Then I whispered to him:

"I'm so scared, Mattias!"

And Mattias hugged me and said:

"I am too!"

Anyway, Jonathan had to promise Orvar that he would ride among the fighting crowd on his horse, to give the other people courage to do what he couldn't or wouldn't do himself.

"The folks of Wild Rose Valley must see you," said Orvar. "They must see both of us."

Then Jonathan said:

"Well, if I must, then I must."

But from the light of the small candle burning in the kitchen, I saw how pale he was.

We had to leave Grim and Fyalar out in the forest with Elfrida, when we came back from Katla Cavern. But it was decided that Sofia would bring them with her, when she rode through the main gate on battle day.

It had also been decided what I would do. I wouldn't do anything, just wait until it was all over. That's what Jonathan said. I would sit completely alone at home in the kitchen and wait.

No one slept much that night.

And then morning came.

Yes, the morning came and battle day, oh, how heart-broken I was that day! I saw and heard more than enough blood and cries, because they fought on the hillside below Mattias's farm. I saw Jonathan riding around there, with the storm tearing at his hair, and all around him there was nothing but fighting and slashing swords and whistling spears and flying arrows and cries and cries. And I said to Fyalar that if Jonathan died, then I wanted to die too.

Yes, I had Fyalar with me in the kitchen. I didn't let anyone know about it, but I needed to have him there. I *couldn't* be alone. Fyalar also looked out through the window at what was happening on the hill outside. He neighed. I didn't know if it was because he wanted to be out with Grim or if he was scared like me.

I was scared...scared, *scared!*

I saw Veder fall in front of Sofia's spear and Kader dropped from Orvar's sword, Dodik too, and many others, they fell left and right. And Jonathan rode among them in the middle, the storm tearing at his hair, and his face became whiter and whiter, and my heart broke more and more.

And then came the end!

Many cries were heard in Wild Rose Valley that day, but one was not like any of the others.

In the middle of the battle a horn sounded through the storm and we heard a cry:

"Katla comes!"

And then came the screams. Katla's screams of hunger that we all knew so well. Then the swords fell down and the spears and arrows, and those who fought couldn't fight anymore. Because they knew that no one could save them. Only the thundering storm and Tengil's battle horn and Katla's cries were now heard in the valley, and Katla's fire poured out killing everyone that Tengil pointed to. He pointed and pointed, and his cruel face was dark with anger, and now the end was coming to Wild Rose Valley, I knew it!

I did not want to watch it, I did not want to watch...not watch anything. Only Jonathan, I needed to know where he was. And I saw him just beyond Mattias's farm. He sat there on Grim, he was pale and completely still and the storm tore at his hair.

"Jonathan," I shouted, "Jonathan, do you hear me?"

But he didn't hear me. And I saw him spur his horse on, and then he flew down the slope, like an arrow he flew, riding quicker than anyone in heaven or on earth, I knew it. He flew toward Tengil...and he flew past him...

And then the battle horn sounded again. But it was Jonathan blowing it now. He had snatched it out of Tengil's hand, and he was blowing it so that it resounded. So that Katla would know she had a new master.

Then it became so quiet. Even the storm ceased. Every one was quiet, and just waited. Tengil sat, insane with fear, on his horse and waited, Katla waited too.

Once again Jonathan blew the horn.

Then Katla screamed and turned in fury on the one she had previously obeyed so blindly.

"Tengil's time will come one day," Jonathan had said, I remembered.

It had come now.

So the battle ended that day in Wild Rose Valley. Many gave their lives for freedom's sake. Yes, it was free now, their valley. But those who were lying there dead didn't know it.

Mattias was dead, I didn't have a grandfather any more. Hubert was dead, he was the first to fall. He never made it through the river gate, because he met Tengil and his soldiers there. He met Katla in front of everyone. Tengil was bringing her that day to punish Wild Rose Valley for the last time, because of Orvar's escape. He hadn't known there would be a battle that day. Though when he found out, he was probably happy to have Katla with him.

But Tengil was dead now, as dead as the others.

"Our tormentor is no more," said Orvar. "Our children shall live in freedom and be happy. Soon Wild Rose Valley will be as before."

But I thought that Wild Rose Valley would never be like before. Not for me. Not without Mattias.

Orvar had received a sword cut across his back, but it was as if he hadn't felt it or didn't care about it. His eyes were still blazing as he talked to the folks in the valley.

"We shall be happy again," he said, time after time.

There were many who cried that day in Wild Rose Valley. But not Orvar.

Sofia lived, she wasn't wounded. And now she would

turn home to Cherry Valley, with all of her soldiers, those who were left alive.

She came to us outside Mattias's farm to say farewell.

"Mattias lived here," she said and cried a little. Then she hugged Jonathan.

"Come home soon to Knights Farm," she said. "I'll think about you every minute, until I see you again."

And then she looked at me.

"Karl, are you coming with me?"

"No," I said, "no, I'll stay with Jonathan!"

I was so scared that Jonathan would send me away with Sofia, but he didn't.

"I really want to have Karl with me," he said.

On the slope below Mattias's farm, Katla was lying like a big terrible lump, silent and covered with blood. Now and then she looked at Jonathan, like a dog looking to see what its master wants. She touched no one now, but as long as she was there, then terror still lay over the valley. No one dared be happy. Wild Rose Valley could neither celebrate its freedom nor mourn its dead, as long as Katla existed, said Orvar. And there was only one who could lead her back to her cave. It was Jonathan.

"Will you help Wild Rose Valley one last time?" asked Orvar. "If you lead her there and chain her, then I'll do the rest, when the time comes."

"Yes," said Jonathan, "I'll help you one last time, Orvar!"

I know how you should travel along the river. You should ride slowly and watch the river flowing down and the glittering water and the willow tree branches dancing in the wind. You shouldn't travel there with a dragon at your heels.

But we did. And we heard the heavy trampling of her feet behind us. Clump, clump, clump, she sounded so dangerous when she walked, Grim and Fyalar almost went crazy. We could hardly control them. Now and then Jonathan blew the horn. It was an awful sound too, and Katla definitely didn't like it. But she had to obey it, when she heard it. It was the only thing that comforted me on our ride.

We didn't say a word to each other, Jonathan and I, we just rode as long as we were able to. Before night and darkness fell, Jonathan had to chain Katla in her cave, where she would die. Then we would never see her again, and we could forget that there was a land called Karmanyaka. The mountains of The Ancient Mountains could stand there for all eternity, but we would never travel this way again, Jonathan had promised me that.

It became still toward evening, no longer stormy, but a calm, warm night. And it was so beautiful when the sun set. It was the kind of evening when you should ride along the river without being scared, I thought.

But I didn't show Jonathan. That I was scared, I mean.

At last we arrived at Karma Falls.

"Karmanyaka, this is the last time you'll see us," said Jonathan as we rode over the bridge. And then he blew the horn.

Katla saw her cliff on the other side of the river. She certainly wanted to go there, because an eager hissing came from her. Right on Grim's hocks, she hissed. She shouldn't have done that.

Because then it happened. Grim shied away, completely terrified and was thrust against the bridge's railing. And I screamed, because I thought Jonathan would go headfirst into Karma Falls. He didn't. But the horn flew out of his hand and vanished down deep in the rushing water.

Katla's cruel eyes had seen everything, and she knew that she no longer had a master. Then she screeched, the fire was already streaming out of her nostrils.

Oh, how we rode to save our miserable lives! How we rode, how we rode! Over the bridge and then up the trail toward Tengil's castle with Katla hissing behind us.

The winding trail zigzagged up through the mountain of The Ancient Mountains. Not even a dream could be this terrible, fleeing from ledge to ledge with Katla after you. Her fire was almost licking our horses' hocks. The flame shot so terribly close to Jonathan. For a horrible moment I thought that he had been burned, but he shouted:

"Don't stop! Ride! Ride!"

Poor Grim and Fyalar, Katla hunted them so that they almost destroyed themselves trying to get away from her. Up through the winding trail, with the lather spraying off them, they were chased faster and faster until they could press on no more. But Katla had fallen behind too, and she screeched with rage. She was in her own territory now, and no one would escape. Her clump, clump, clump increased in speed, and I knew that she would win in the end. Because of her stubborn cruelty.

Far, far we rode, and I had no hope of us being rescued.

We had reached quite a way up the mountain. We still had the lead, and we saw Katla right under us on the path, along the narrow rock ledge over Karma Falls. And she stood there for a while. Because this was her cliff. It was where she used to stand and stare, and that's what she did now, too. Almost reluctantly she stopped and stared down into the falls, fire and smoke spouted forth from her nostrils, and she stomped impatiently back and forth. But then she remembered us, and she glared up at us with blazing eyes.

You're cruel, I thought, you're cruel, cruel. Why don't you stay there on your cliff?

But I knew that she would come. She would come…

Finally we reached the great stone where we had seen her stretch out her horrible head, the first time we came to Karmanyaka. And now, suddenly, our horses had no energy to go farther. It's awful, when your horse collapses underneath you. But that's what happened. Grim and Fyalar just collapsed down onto the path. And before, if we had hoped for a miracle to save us, it was clear there was no hope now.

We had lost, we knew it. And Katla knew it too. A devilish triumph came to her eyes! She stood still on her cliff and glared up at us. I thought that she laughed scornfully. She wasn't in a hurry now. It was as if she thought: I'll come when I come! Now you can wait!

Jonathan looked at me kindly as he always did.

"Forgive me, Scotty, for dropping the horn," he said. "But I couldn't help it."

I wanted to tell Jonathan that I never, never, never had anything to forgive him for, but I was numb with terror.

Katla stood down there. Fire and smoke gusting out of her nostrils, and her feet began stomping. We stood sheltered behind the great stone so that her fire couldn't reach us. I clung to Jonathan, oh, how I clung to him, and he looked at me with tears in his eyes.

Then rage overtook him. He leaned out and shouted to Katla down there:

"Don't you touch Scotty! Do you hear me, you monster, don't you touch Scotty, or else…"

He gripped the stone as if he were a giant and could frighten her. He wasn't a giant and he couldn't frighten Katla. But the stone was lying loose beyond reach of her fire.

"Neither spears nor arrows nor swords can hurt Katla," Orvar had said. He should have also said that a great stone wouldn't do anything either, however large it was.

Katla didn't die from the stone that Jonathan overturned down onto her. But it landed right on her. And with a shriek that could tumble a mountain, she fell backward into Karma Falls.

CHAPTER SIXTEEN

N O, JONATHAN DIDN'T KILL KATLA. KARM DID. AND
Katla killed Karm. In front of our eyes. We saw it.
No one other than Jonathan and I have seen two monsters from ancient times destroy each other. We saw
them fight each other to the death in Karma Falls.

When Katla cried out and disappeared, at first we
couldn't believe it. We couldn't believe that she was really
gone. Where she sank, we only saw swirling froth.
Nothing more. No Katla.

But then we saw the serpent. He raised his green
head up out of the froth, and his tail whipped at the
water, oh, he was horrible, a giant serpent, as long as the
river was wide, exactly as Elfrida had said.

The serpent of Karma Falls, which she had heard
sagas about when she was little, he was no more a saga
than Katla. He did exist and was a monster as terrible as
Katla. His head turned in every direction, he searched…
and he saw Katla. She rose up out of the chasm and suddenly she was in the middle of the whirling water, and

the twisting serpent threw himself over her and coiled around her. She spurted her deadly fire toward him, but he clung tightly to her, extinguishing the fire in her chest. Then she slashed at him, and he slashed her back. They slashed and bit, both of them wanting to kill. They had longed for this since ancient times, yes, they slashed and bit like two furious creatures, hurling their horrible bodies at each other in the whirling water. Katla shrieked between bites, but Karm slashed in complete silence, and black dragon blood and green serpent blood flowed out into the white froth and colored it dark with their foulness.

How long did they hold on? It felt as if I had stood there on the path for a thousand years and never saw anything other than these two raging monsters in their final battle.

It was a long and horrible fight, but it ended at last. A piercing cry came from Katla, it was her death cry, then she went silent. By then Karm no longer had his head. But his body didn't let go of her, and they sank together, tightly entwined, down into the depths. And then there was no Karm and no Katla, they were gone as if they had never existed. The froth was white again and the poisonous blood from the monsters was washed away by the mighty waters of Karma Falls. Everything was as before. Like it had been since ancient times.

We stood there gasping on the path, although it was all over. We couldn't speak for a long time. But at last Jonathan said:

"We must get out of here! Quickly! It'll be dark soon, and I don't want night to fall on us in Karmanyaka."

Poor Grim and Fyalar! I don't know how we got them on their feet and how we left. They were so tired that they could scarcely lift their legs.

But we left Karmanyaka and rode over the bridge for the last time. Then the horses weren't able to take a step farther. As soon as we reached the foot of the bridge on the other side, they dropped down and remained lying there. It was as if they thought, now we've helped you to Nangiyala and that's enough!

"We'll make a campfire at our old place," said Jonathan. He meant the rock ledge where we stayed during the thunderstorm, when I saw Katla for the first time. I still shivered when I thought about it, and I would've rather camped for the night in some other place. But we couldn't go farther now.

The horses needed water first, before we could settle down for the night. We gave them water, but they didn't want to drink. They were too tired. Then I became anxious.

"Jonathan, there's something odd about them," I said. "Do you think they'll be better when they've gotten some sleep?"

"Yes, everything will be fine when they've gotten some sleep," said Jonathan.

I pet Fyalar, he was lying there with his eyes closed.

"What a day you've had, poor Fyalar," I said. "But tomorrow everything will be fine, that's what Jonathan said."

We made our fire right where we'd had our first one. And that cliff where we withstood the thunderstorm really was the finest place you could think of for a campfire, if you could just forget that Karmanyaka was so close. Behind us were high mountain walls, they were still warm from the sun and protected us from all the wind. In front of us the cliff dropped straight down into Karma Falls, and on the side closest to the foot of the bridge there was also a steep slope down toward a green meadow. It appeared just as a little green spot far, far below us.

We sat by our fire and watched the twilight fall over the mountains of The Ancient Mountains and the river of the Ancient Rivers. I was tired and I thought that I had never lived through a longer or more difficult day. From dawn to dusk there hadn't been anything other than blood and terror and death. There were some adventures that should not happen, Jonathan had once said, and we'd had more than enough of them this day. The day of battle — it had been very long and difficult, but now it was finally over.

Yet our sorrow wasn't gone. I thought of Mattias. I mourned for him so much, and while we sat there by the fire, I asked Jonathan:

"Where do you think Mattias is now?"

"He's in Nangilima," said Jonathan.

"Nangilima, I've never heard you talk about that," I said.

"Yes, you have," said Jonathan. "Don't you remember the morning when I left Cherry Valley and you were so scared? Don't you remember what I said then: 'If I don't come back, we'll meet in Nangilima.' And Mattias is there now."

Then he told me about Nangilima. He hadn't told me any stories in a long time, we hadn't had the time.

But now while he sat there by the fire and talked about Nangilima, it was almost like he was sitting next to my sofa in the kitchen back at home in town.

"In Nangilima…in Nangilima," said Jonathan with that voice he always used, when he told stories. "It's still during the time of campfires and sagas there."

"Poor Mattias, if it's full of adventures that should not happen," I said.

But Jonathan said that in Nangilima it was not a time of cruel sagas, but only happy ones that were full of play. People played there, well, they worked too, of course, and helped each other with everything, but they played a lot and sang and danced and told sagas, he said. Sometimes they frightened the children with very cruel, horrible sagas about monsters like Karm and Katla and cruel people like Tengil. But afterward they laughed at it.

"Are you scared now?" they said to the children. "It's only a story. Something that never happened. Never here in our valley at least."

Mattias had it good in Nangilima said Jonathan. He had an old farm in Apple Valley, it was the most beautiful farm in the prettiest and greenest of Nangilima's valleys.

"Soon it will be time to pick the apples in his apple orchard," said Jonathan. "We should be there to help him. He's too old to climb up a ladder."

"I almost wish that we could go there," I said. Because I thought that is sounded so fine there in Nangilima, and I longed for Mattias.

"Why do you say that?" said Jonathan. "Well, we could live with Mattias. At Mattias's farm in Apple Valley in Nangilima."

226

"Tell me how it would be," I said.

"Oh, it would be fine," said Jonathan. "We could ride around the forest and make our campfires here and there — if only you knew what the forests around Nangilima's valleys were like! And deep in the forest lie clear little lakes. We could make a campfire by a new lake every evening and be away for days and nights and then go home to Mattias again."

"And help him with the apples," I said. "But then Sofia and Orvar would have to look after Cherry Valley and Wild Rose Valley without you, Jonathan."

"Well, why not?" said Jonathan. "Sofia and Orvar don't need me any longer, they can set things straight in their valleys."

But then he became quiet and didn't talk any more. We were silent, both of us, and I was tired and not happy at all. It wasn't comforting to hear about Nangilima, which was so far away from us.

The darkness grew more and more, and the mountains became blacker and blacker. Large black birds hovered over us and they cried so forlornly, everything felt melancholy. Karma Falls roared, I was tired of listening to it. It made me remember what I wanted to forget. Sad, everything was sad, and I thought I'd probably never be happy again.

I moved closer to Jonathan. He sat so still, leaning against the mountain wall, and his face was pale. He looked like a prince in a saga, as he sat there, but he was a pale and tired prince. Poor Jonathan, you aren't happy either, I thought, oh, if I could just make you a little happy!

As we were sitting there in silence, Jonathan said:

"Scotty, there is something I must tell you!"

I became scared at once, because when he said that, it was always something sad that he wanted to tell me.

"What do you need to talk about?" I asked.

He stroked my cheek with his forefinger.

"Don't be scared, Scotty...but do you remember what Orvar said? Even a little flame from Katla's fire is enough to paralyze or kill anyone, do you remember him saying that?"

"Yes, but why are talking about it now?" I asked.

"Because..." said Jonathan. "Because a little flame from Katla's fire burned me, as we fled from her."

My heart had been broken all day from the grief and fear, but I hadn't cried. Now the tears came from me almost as a scream.

"Will you die again now, Jonathan?" I cried. And then Jonathan said:

"No! But that's what I would want to do. Because I'll never move again."

He explained to me the cruelty of Katla's fire. If it didn't kill, then it did something much worse. It destroyed something inside, so that you were paralyzed. It wasn't noticeable immediately, but it came sneaking up, slowly and unrelentingly.

"I can only move my arms now," he said. "And soon I won't be able to do that either."

"But don't you think it will go away?" I said, crying.

"No, Scotty, it will never go away," said Jonathan. "Unless I can go to Nangilima!"

Unless he could go to Nangilima, oh, now I understood!

He was thinking of leaving me alone again, I knew it! One time he had disappeared to Nangiyala without me...

"But not this time," I cried. "Not without me! You're not going to disappear to Nangilima without me!"

"Do you want to come with me, then?" he asked.

"Yes, what do you think?" I said. "Haven't I said, that wherever you go, I'll follow!"

"You've said that, and it's my comfort," said Jonathan. "But it's a difficult task to get there!"

He sat quietly for a while again, and then he said:

"Do you remember the time, when we jumped? That horrible time when it was burning and we jumped down into the yard. I came to Nangiyala then, do you remember that?"

"Do I remember it?" I said and cried even more. "How can you ask that? Don't you think that I've remembered it every moment since then?"

"Yes, I know," said Jonathan and he stroked my cheek again. And then he said:

"I think that we might be able to jump once more. Down the slope there. Down into the meadow."

"Well, then we'll die," I said. "But will we go to Nangilima?"

"Yes, you can be sure of it," said Jonathan. "As soon as we land, we'll already see the light from Nangilima. We'll see the morning light over Nangilima's valleys, yes, because it is morning there now."

"Haha, we can jump right into Nangilima," I said and laughed for the first time in a long while.

"That we can," said Jonathan. "And as soon as we land, we'll also see the path to Apple Valley right in front of us. And Grim and Fyalar are already standing there and waiting. We only need to get into the saddle and trot off."

"And you won't be paralyzed at all then," I said.

"No, then I'll be free of all evil and so happy that I won't know what to do! And you too, Scotty, you'll also be happy there. The path to Apple Valley goes through the forest. How do you think it will feel, as we ride there in the morning sun, you and I?"

"Good," I said and laughed again.

"And we won't be in a hurry," said Jonathan. "We can swim in a little lake, if we want. We'll still have time to reach Apple Valley before Mattias has soup ready."

"How happy he'll be, when we arrive," I said. But then it was as if I had been hit by a club. Grim and Fyalar, how could Jonathan believe that we could take them with us to Nangilima?

230

"How can you say that they're already standing there waiting for us? They're lying over there asleep."

"They're not sleeping, Scotty! They're dead. From Katla's fire. But what you see over there are just their shells. Believe me, Grim and Fyalar are already standing by the path to Nangilima, waiting for us."

"Let's hurry then," I said. "So they don't need to wait any longer."

Then Jonathan laughed at me and smiled.

"I can't hurry at all," he said. "I can't leave this spot, have you forgotten?"

And then I realized what I must do.

"Jonathan, I'll take you on my back," I said. "You did it for me once. And now I'll do it for you. It's only fair."

"Yes, that's fair," said Jonathan. "But do you think you dare, Scotty Lionheart?"

I went over to the slope and looked down. It was already so dark. You could hardly see the meadow any longer. But it was such a steep drop that it was terrifying beyond belief. If we jumped there, at least we'd be certain of getting to Nangilima, both of us. No one needed to be left alone to lie mourning and crying and being scared.

But *we* would not jump, *I* would do it. It was a hard task to get to Nangilima, Jonathan had said, and now for the first time I realized why. How would I dare, how would I ever dare?

Well, if you won't risk it now, I thought, then you're a piece of dirt and you'll never be anything other than a piece of dirt.

I went back to Jonathan.

"Yes, I dare," I said.

"Brave little Scotty," he said. "Then we'll do it now!"

"I want to sit for a while with you first," I said.

"Just not for long," said Jonathan.

"No, just until it becomes completely dark," I said. "So I can't see anything."

And I sat next to him and held his hand and felt that he was strong and good, through and through, and that nothing was really dangerous, with him there.

The night and darkness came over Nangiyala, over the mountains and rivers and land. And I stood by the slope with Jonathan, he clung tightly to me with his arms around my neck, and I felt his breath behind my ear. He was breathing quite calmly. Not like me...Jonathan, my brother, why am I not as brave as you?

I didn't see the steep slope in front of me, but I knew that it was there. And I just needed to take a step out into the darkness, then it would all be over. It would go so quickly.

"Scotty Lionheart," said Jonathan, "are you scared?"

"No...yes, I am scared! But I'll still do it, Jonathan, I'll do it now...now...and then I'll never be scared any more. Never be sca..."

"Oh, Nangilima! Yes, Jonathan, yes, I see the light! *I see the light!*"